POLITICAL POLLING

Campaigning American Style

Series Editors
Daniel M. Shea, Allegheny College
F. Christopher Arterton, George Washington University

Few areas of American politics have changed as dramatically in recent times as the way in which we choose public officials. Students of politics and political communications are struggling to keep abreast of these developments—and the 2000 and 2002 elections only feed the confusion and concern. *Campaigning American Style* is a new series of books devoted to both the theory and practice of American electoral politics. It offers high quality work on the conduct of new-style electioneering and how it is transforming our electoral system. Scholars, practitioners, and students of campaigns and elections need new resources to keep pace with the rapid rate of electoral change, and we are pleased to help provide them in this exciting series.

Titles in the Series

Campaign Mode: Strategic Vision in Congressional Elections
by Michael John Burton and Daniel M. Shea

The Civic Web: Online Politics and Democratic Values
edited by David M. Anderson and Michael Cornfield

High-Tech Grass Roots: The Professionalization of Local Elections
by J. Cherie Strachan

Political Polling: Strategic Information in Campaigns
by Jeffrey M. Stonecash

Forthcoming

Life After Reform: When the Bipartisan Campaign Reform Act Meets Politics
edited by Michael J. Malbin

The Rules: Election Regulations in the American States
by Costas Panagopoulos

Negative Campaigning
by Richard R. Lau and Gerald M. Pomper

POLITICAL POLLING

Strategic Information in Campaigns

JEFFREY M. STONECASH

ROWMAN & LITTLEFIELD PUBLISHERS, INC.
Lanham • Boulder • New York • Oxford

ROWMAN & LITTLEFIELD PUBLISHERS, INC.

Published in the United States of America
by Rowman & Littlefield Publishers, Inc.
A Member of the Rowman & Littlefield Publishing Group
4501 Forbes Boulevard, Suite 200, Lanham, Maryland 20706
www.rowmanlittlefield.com

PO Box 317
Oxford
OX2 9RU, UK

British Library Cataloguing in Publication Information Available

Library of Congress Cataloging-in-Publication Data

Stonecash, Jeffrey M.
    Political polling : strategic information in campaigns / Jeffrey M.
Stonecash.
        p. cm.
    Includes bibliographical references and index.
    ISBN 0-7425-2552-X (cloth : alk. paper)—
    ISBN 0-7425-2553-8 (pbk. : alk. paper)
    1. Campaign management—United States.   2. Political campaigns—United
States.   3. Public opinion polls.   I. Title.
JK2281 .S76 2003
324.7—dc21   2002153364

Printed in the United States of America

♾ ™ The paper used in this publication meets the minimum requirements of
American National Standard for Information Sciences—Permanence of Paper for
Printed Library Materials, ANSI/NISO Z39.48-1992.

CONTENTS

Preface   vii

1 Campaigns, Democracy, and the Need for Information   1

2 Purposes, Limited Budgets, and When to Poll   11

3 What Kind of Poll?   21

4 Writing Questions: Language and the Script   27

5 Pulling a Sample: Who Votes, Sample Size, and
   Representativeness   59

6 Callers and Calling   73

7 The Crucial Part: Analysis and Developing a Campaign
   Plan   79

8 Reports and Recommendations   117

9 Tracking Polls and the Undecided   127

10 A Final Note on Polling and Democracy   141

Appendix: A Sample Report   145

Bibliography   161

Index   167

About the Author   169

PREFACE

POLLING IS CRUCIAL for conducting campaigns. The purpose of this book is to explain how campaigns decide what polling information to gather and how to use that information to help candidates win elections. In addition, the book explains how campaign polling is done. Poll results tell candidates where they stand: how well known they are, who knows them, and what people think of them. Polls also tell candidates about the opinions of the electorate, who holds those opinions, and how people with differing opinions are likely to vote. The challenge for a pollster is to interpret this information and tell a candidate how to deal with the electorate to win an election.

While the emphasis here is on how to use information, an equally central concern is the interaction between candidates, polling, and the messages presented to the electorate. It is widely presumed that polls determine the positions candidates adopt. Quite the contrary, polling lets candidates know which of their *already existing* views they should emphasize and which they should not emphasize. How that process works will be addressed throughout.

Author Background

I have been conducting polls for eighteen years. I began in 1985 with telephone and exit polls for a local television station, when another faculty member, Tom Patterson, had had enough of exit polling. I was lucky enough to precisely predict several very prominent local races. That prompted one local politician, Jim Walsh, to have lunch with me to discuss polling. He went on to run in a primary for county executive, for which I did the polling. He was fortunate enough to lose by thirty-three votes, and he was then well known and available to run for the local seat in Congress when it opened up the next year. He has been in the House of Representatives since 1988. He gave me a start in polling and has been a wonderful individual to work for since then. He gave me a start and tolerated some mistakes, and I greatly appreciate the opportunity to work with him. That led to other work, for both Democrats and Republicans. It also led to working with Jack Cookfair, who handles television and radio ads. Working with him has taught me a great deal about how to write scripts to gather information that is useful for campaigns. I greatly appreciate what I have learned.

Since then I have done polling for members of Congress, state legislators, county executives and mayors, county and city comptrollers, district attorneys, county legislators and city council members, and village mayors. My polling is split between Democrats and Republicans, which is highly unusual. I have also done polling for county and town party organizations. I handle all aspects of the process, from meeting with the candidates and designing the initial survey, analyzing voter registration files and pulling a sample, training college students as callers and supervising the calling, analyzing results, and writing a report and making recommendations to the candidate, the campaign staff, and those creating ads and direct mail. I also conduct surveys for nonprofit groups, businesses, universities, and local governments. The work has given me an invaluable political education. It has provided me with a continuing education in the dynamics of campaigns and the role of issues in campaigns.

At about the same time I began working on campaigns, I joined the New York Assembly Intern Program as the Professor-in-Residence to teach a course on New York politics to interns. The need to interpret annual party interactions in the legislature has also been an invaluable prod to understand politics. The weekly conversations with Jim Murphy, the Director of the Intern Program, and Robert Pecorella, the other Professor-in-Residence, have been a great ongoing seminar in politics.

I could not have developed any expertise in polling and conducted polling without the support of my department and the Maxwell School, the social science school of Syracuse University. Engaging in an applied political activity like polling might be seen in some places as "just consulting" and not of educational value. Thankfully, Maxwell is a place that has a positive view of having someone around who is involved in campaigns. I am thankful for that and appreciate the understanding.

Finally, Mark Brewer provided a very valuable reading of the manuscript. As always, his comments are right on the mark. I appreciate the suggestions.

The Ethics of Polling

What follows focuses on the polling process. It may be appropriate before beginning that discussion to comment on the ethics of polling. When you work for a candidate, you are hired for your expertise, and your job is to help the candidate win. There are still some general rules that a pollster should follow.

Focus on providing information and never get too close to your client. You may become friends with the candidate, but your job is not to befriend him. Your job is to provide accurate information to the candidate, even if it is bad news. When news is bad, there is often a tendency to kill the messenger. The pollster's job is to be prepared for that reaction and not flinch from providing that information because you are a friend of the candidate. Your job is to tell the candidate how she is coming across to the electorate and how the person's message is being received. Getting too close to someone can make it more difficult to provide blunt advice.

Avoid life "inside" the campaign office. A pollster is concerned with how the general public sees the candidates and issues. The campaign office is filled with stories of how political insiders and various elected officials are relating to each other. It is a world that has nothing to do with how the public sees things. People involved in politics know a great deal about candidates, issues, and political connections. They often presume that others have this same level of familiarity, and they are initially skeptical when a pollster tells them that not many people know them, that a seemingly prominent issue is largely unperceived by the public, and that news stories about something have not registered with the public. It is important to not lapse into these presumptions of awareness, which can occur if a pollster spends a lot of time in conversation with insiders. It is also important not to get drawn into the "palace intrigues" of what insiders are in support or not in support of a candidate. These inside games do not matter to the public, and the pollster should stay focused on the public. Distance from the inside operations is a virtue.

Do not allow yourself to become partisan. The people who work in campaigns hold partisan views. They believe in their ideas and sometimes find it hard to believe that others do not. After all, most of their acquaintances agree with them. That partisanship often makes it hard for them to see the other side and to see the need to think about how the other side's argument will work. Many partisans cannot imagine that ideological criticisms from an opponent will work. It is important not to get caught up in that view and presume an impact or nonimpact without checking. It is the job of the pollster to keep an empirical focus to discussions and not endorse partisan presumptions that various views could not possible be accepted. During the impeachment proceedings of Bill Clinton, it became very clear, listening to both sides, that each side was in disbelief of the views of the other. A pollster should avoid becoming committed to either side and help the campaign remain focused on "what is."

Do not allow biased questions. The goal is to get accurate information. It does the candidate no good if you ask biased questions. Your report and script may also be seen by others, and it will do your reputation no good if you let candidates ask biased questions. Others will think the questions are your choice.

Keep your mouth shut and don't talk with the press. Those who want publicity should run for office and not be pollsters. It invariably leads to trouble when pollsters start talking to the press. If your focus is on accurate information and being direct, those skills are not good training for dealing with journalists, who are always trying to gather inside information about the campaign. Your candor can come back to embarrass you as undesired quotes in a newspaper story.

Do not share poll results without permission. The results you gather are paid for by the campaign. They are not yours, and it is inappropriate for you to do favors for others, unless the candidate approves the sharing of information. If other candidates are to eventually receive information on their name recognition, for example, the candidate paying for the poll should get all credit for providing that information.

Jeffrey M. Stonecash
Syracuse, New York

Campaigns, Democracy, and the Need for Information

Polls and Democracy

THERE IS SEEMINGLY LITTLE POSITIVE to say about political polling. Critics argue that it serves either to undermine political leadership and character or to provide the means for politicians to manipulate the electorate. Either way, polling is corrupting democracy. The more conventional argument is the former. The essence of the argument is that democracy needs politicians who lead and polls encourage politicians to pander to the public and become poll driven (Fishkin 1996). Rather than formulate policy plans and lead public opinion, politicians are seen as responding to the opinions found in polls, even while proclaiming that they are leaders. When campaigning in 2002, George W. Bush "promised to govern 'based upon principles and not polls and focus groups.'" His advisors argued that "Mr. Bush avoids using surveys to put politics over principles" (Hallow 2002, 1–2). Despite that, in May 2002, the *New York Times* reported the following on the front page:

> It was only in January that Karl Rove, President Bush's chief political strategist, was telling Republican operatives to trumpet the administration's handling of the war on terrorism as a major selling point in the November midterm elections.
>
> But now, in a striking readjustment driven by several recent polls, Republican strategists are warning that the war will not guarantee their party victory this fall, and that President Bush has responded with a significant refocusing of what political analysts call the "Mommy issues" of his domestic agenda. (Bumiller 2002, A1)[1]

By most accounts, Bill Clinton was worse than George W. Bush. Dick Morris, former Clinton White House advisor, said that "Clinton

had me poll every week and, during times of intense political controversy, he had me poll every night." "Mr. Clinton was often criticized
for using polls like a moistened finger in the wind—to test what initia-
tives the public might be in the mood for, without regard for political
principle (Hallow 2002, 1). The essential criticism is that polls are
leading to poll-driven policy choices (King 1997, 44). As Elizabeth
Drew, a frequent writer about politics, put it regarding Bill Clinton:

> If the definition of leadership is acting on things one feels
> strongly about and being willing to risk some political capital
> in order to achieve them—Clinton has come up short. In
> fact, with few exceptions, it wasn't very clear what Clinton
> did feel strongly about. No presidency has been as poll-
> driven as Bill Clinton's. . . . A Democratic political consultant
> says, "Reagan used polling to figure out how to sell his
> beliefs. Clinton used polling to figure out what to believe."
> (Drew 1999, 1–2)

While these observers see a clear degree of difference between these
two men, both presidents have engaged in strategic political behavior
to improve their electoral standing. That is, they seek to respond to
public opinion with policy proposals that please the electorate. The
presumption is that politicians "find out what they [the electorate]
want and feed it back to them." This view fits with the growing practice among journalists to see and report campaigns and elections in
strategic terms. Over the last forty years, there has been a steady
increase in the percentage of media stories that operate from a perspective that politicians adopt positions as a means to secure more
votes and not out of a sincere desire to enact a particular policy (Patterson 1994, 72–75).

The implications of this view are troubling, because of what they
suggest about how the democratic process is being changed. If politicians are pandering, then there is little likelihood they will propose
policies that will be ahead of voters. While more and more Americans
buy less efficient SUVs, and gasoline consumption and reliance on for-
eign oil continues to increase, politicians are unlikely to suggest that
voters should be forced to change their habits because it will risk alienating a large bloc of voters. The electorate is disinclined to change

their views, so change becomes unlikely, even if there are credible arguments that change is necessary.

While this view denigrates polling because of how it leads politicians to slavishly follow public opinion, others see polling and focus groups as dangerous because they provide a means to manipulate public opinion. In recent years politics has become more polarized. Democrats and Republicans in Congress are more likely to have different constituencies and to vote against each other. The electoral bases of the two parties now differ more by race (Carmines and Stimson 1989), ideology (Abramowitz 1994; Abramowitz and Saunders 1998), and class (Stonecash 2000), than they did twenty to thirty years ago. Elected officials draw on more sharply divided and distinct sets of core supporters, and they vote differently from each other (Groseclose, et al. 1999; Stonecash, Brewer, and Mariani 2002). Elected officials are now faced with intense core supporters with policy preferences that tend to be either very liberal or very conservative, and not moderate. Faced with these strong and more extreme pressures, politicians seek to find ways to respond to their core supporters.

This situation prompts politicians to use polls and focus groups to try to find language for discussing policy proposals that will allow them to sound as if they are responding to the majority while still voting to please their core supporters (Jacobs and Shapiro 2000). The goal is to find language that will allow them to distort what they do. For example, taxes are a consistent concern. Republican supporters think they are too high and the affluent pay too much in taxes. Democratic supporters think the rich evade too much in the way of taxes. The reality is that over the last twenty years the more affluent have come to pay a larger portion of all federal income taxes (because they make more of all income earned) and tax rates on the less affluent have been cut (Stonecash and Milstein 2001). At the same time, the Social Security tax has come to comprise a larger portion of all taxes paid. Workers pay a flat rate for this tax, up to some maximum income level of approximately $87,000, with the result that the very affluent pay a smaller percentage of their income for this tax. That is, they pay no tax on income from $87,000 and up. This tax then imposes a greater burden on those with lower to middle incomes, raising the overall tax burden on those with lower to middle incomes. Republican members of Congress, seeking to justify income tax cuts to respond to their more affluent supporters and those who dislike taxes in principle, do not want to talk about the issue of tax burdens by income level when all taxes (income, Social Security, Medicare) are included, because that comparison shows the less affluent paying a higher percentage of their income in taxes.

Republican members of Congress then use focus groups to find that a majority of voters like the language of "giving people back the money they earned." They then conduct polls with questions that push people into simplistic alternatives such as "do people who earned money deserve to get their money back or don't they?" Their poll results show many people agree with the statement, so this allows them to simplify and distort the issue. Democrats find it hard to disagree that people do not deserve to have money they earned, and there is little discussion about larger policy goals the society might pursue. This presentation of the issue gives the Republicans language that allows them to justify a tax cut. Democrats, not to be outdone in such tactics, do not want to discuss the fact that the affluent provide a larger portion of all income tax revenue, so they use the same approach to end up focusing on the percentage of the cut going to the rich, because this caters to their liberal core constituency. They conduct polls asking "Do the rich pay too little in taxes?" Each side finds questions that cater to their constituency and for which a majority may agree with the question. The result is a distorted policy debate, in which there is little discussion of how the tax system has changed over time, but the core constituents of both parties are pleased that their view is being forcefully articulated. Polling contributes to this by allowing the parties to pursue arguments that serve only their side.

In short, there are reasons to worry about the effects of polling on democracy. Either it leads to timid politicians simply following the public, or it provides a tool for politicians to find a way to distort public debates to appease a polarized electorate. There are reasons to wonder if the emergence of widespread and frequent polling is advancing democracy.

A More Realistic View of Politicians and Polling

The argument of this book is that these negative views of political polling are largely wrong. The opposing arguments that polls drive politicians or that politicians use polls to find ways to distort issues and manipulate public opinion both have problems. First, the arguments enormously simplify the situation of politicians. Politicians are rarely in the position of just responding to opinion or just trying to shape opinion. As often happens in debates, this is a false dichotomy in which neither alternative captures reality very well. Elected officials are regularly trying to balance numerous pressures, and they respond in multiple ways to the electorate.

With regard to responding to the public, multiple responses are possible, depending on the situation. In some cases politicians see opinion as relatively set, and when faced with an intense majority in their jurisdiction, most recognize the need to respond. While many politicians might like to change Social Security (who receives a full amount, how the cost of living is calculated, when eligibility begins, etc.), most recognize that it has become, at least in the short run, seen as a right, and it is difficult to discuss altering it. On other issues, opinions are unformed, unstable, in flux, or complex, and politicians may recognize that they have considerable flexibility in how they respond. Environmental enforcement issues are complex, often involving technical issues. While the electorate consistently indicates strong support for tough environmental enforcement regulations (Dunlap 2002, 10–14), many politicians are aware that the electorate is relatively unaware of exactly what the policy options are or mean, and what enforcement actually occurs. This gives them leeway to pursue more stringent or lax enforcement. On some issues, it is clear that how the question is asked significantly affects public reactions, so politicians are aware that there is not a clear and stable public opinion out there. When President Clinton was trying to enact universal health care in 1993, many polls asked if there was a crisis in health care, and majorities chose yes. Republicans eventually asked two different questions. They asked if people wanted to choose their own doctor or let government choose their doctor. A strong majority wanted to choose their own doctor. The second question was whether each individual was satisfied with his or her own health care arrangement. A majority answered that they were. The reality was that there was not "a" public opinion that politicians had to respond to. This same lack of clarity about what is public opinion occurs for other issues.

Further, politicians have their own views, some of them strong and some of them less set and evolving. In areas in which their views are relatively set, they may believe they are doing the right thing, and they may be willing to work long and hard to achieve policy change in areas in which they have strong convictions. They may also recognize that some occasions are more appropriate for strong advocacy for an issue they support. At other times they may see the need to wait until conditions improve. When new issues emerge and politicians have not developed their own views, the polling data lets them know how the public sees the situation, depending on how the question is worded. In most of these situations, the official realizes that the situation is new and in flux and that there is time to think about the issue and work out a viewpoint while listening to the different polling results generated. Few just adopt the position generated in the latest poll.

Finally, politicians are always trying to balance the interests of different groups. They worry about their image among the general electorate, and they also worry about their image among core supporters. Balancing their statements and behavior to try to please both is a continual challenge. An assertion that politicians are slaves to public opinion may make for a provocative statement and an interesting argument, but it does not represent the situation politicians really face.

With regard to politicians trying to shape opinion, most do not have the resources to engage in the intense process of running numerous television and radio ads and then conducting regular polls to track the impact of their message. Most politicians do not have the money to poll extensively or to advertise so frequently that they can shape opinions. With regard to polling, it costs money and most campaigns have fairly limited polling budgets, and most cannot afford to do the polling that would be necessary to closely track public opinion or test campaign themes. Presidential candidates and a few U.S. senators can afford this, but whatever success presidents have in leading public opinion does not capture the situations of the overwhelming bulk of elected officials. For most politicians, polling can only be done periodically, making it difficult to engage in the repeated and detailed polling necessary to assess the effect of every strategic move.

Even if candidates could poll often enough, they rarely have the access to free media (via news conferences and press stories) and the money for campaign ads to focus on shaping issues. Most advertising goes for building name identification and defining the candidate. It would be an enormous luxury for most campaigns to move to trying to shape public opinion. If candidates even contemplated that move, they would also face the reality of crowded airwaves, with many other candidates issuing messages.

There are also problems with the specific arguments about how polling plays a role in campaigns. As for the notion that candidates simply follow public opinion, politicians rarely use polling to decide what to support. They use polling to tell them what to stress of the views they already have. Most politicians begin with opinions about issues. On those issues that they have opinions about, politicians are concerned with how compatible their views are with those of particular groups of voters. If their electoral base supports them on five of seven issues, then their concern is to stress those five issues and call much less attention to the other two positions. For issues that create problems, the goal of polling is to tell them how they might present the positions they have. It is rare for politicians to reverse a position they have taken because of what a poll indicates. When it does happen, it is so infrequent that it is news. There is little evidence to support the fundamental presumptions of critics that polling drives policy positions. It may drive how an issue is presented, as will be discussed, but it does not determine whether a candidate takes liberal or conservative policy positions.

My experience has been that when politicians do hold opinions that diverge from the majority of their constituents (though perhaps not from their core supporters), the biggest challenge is to persuade them that it might be wise to deemphasize those views in favor of other concerns. These efforts at persuasion are often difficult. Politicians usually come to office with developed views, and they believe in their views. They are not eager to stifle their beliefs.

Even on new issues—those not previously part of public discussions—polling does not create a politician's position. Most politicians have preexisting views of the role of government, of how much business should be regulated, of how much inequality should be addressed, and so on. When a new issue emerges, the role of polling is to provide information to politicians about how the issue is seen, how different options are seen, and to allow them to track how the issue is developing over time.

The alternative view, that politicians use polling to help them find phrases that can be used to manipulate the public, also has limitations. Again, most politicians begin with existing views of issues and notions of how to present their arguments to the public. Polling may help them sort out which ones best connect with the electorate, but few begin without some initial notion of how they can best present an idea. If conservatives think that regulation of the health insurance industry is bad, they were probably already inclined to think that the basic principle is the right of people to choose their own doctor. A poll may confirm that, but the idea is not a simple creation of a pollster.

Information and Its Uses

What, then, is polling used for? Polling information is used by politicians to help them understand the public. It helps them understand their constituency, rather than pander to it. Indeed, there is an argument to be made that polling contributes to democracy by providing politicians with a greater sense of the concerns of their electorate than was possible before.

Candidates and campaign managers need information on several basic matters. They need to know how they are seen by the electorate and how a possible or actual opponent is seen. They need to know the demographic characteristics of the population in the political jurisdiction. They need to know the opinions of the likely electorate, who holds what opinions, and how those opinions affect vote choices. All this information provides the means to determine a candidate's chances of winning an election.

The most basic information that a politician needs to know is how she is seen. What percentage of voters has heard of her? Is the electorate's impression of her favorable or unfavorable? How well known is a probable opponent, and what impression does the electorate have of that opponent? Which groups in the electorate know the candidates more, and which groups hold favorable and unfavorable views of the candidates? Does her own party have a positive view of her and how well does she fare among Independents? Is she connecting with her party base, and do they support her? How is she seen by Independents? Where does the opponent stand on these matters? How close is a matchup of the candidates, and who supports each candidate?

This information allows candidates to determine how much money they need to raise and how they should spend it. If the candidate has low name recognition, then more money is necessary for television ads and literature that will increase her name recognition. If she is failing to get her message across to the voters she needs to attract, money has to be spent getting a targeted message to those specific voters likely to be receptive to it. All of these decisions start with knowing how the candidates are seen and who supports which candidate. That requires polling.

Candidates need to know what issues are important and what electoral groups hold what opinions. Do voters whom the candidate should attract hold the same views as she does? If so, has she made this issue connection with voters so those holding similar views choose her in a matchup? If not, money has to be spent communicating her policy positions so that voters with specific views see her as the person best suited to pursue their goals. Are there issues that will cause the candidate problems? Is much of the district pro-choice, while the candidate is not? Does the opponent hold positions that conflict with his electoral base, such that ads might be run to pull voters away from him? Each candidate needs to know which issues she can emphasize to try to build support and which issues she can use to criticize an opponent to reduce his vote total.

Without this information, campaigns become guessing games. Campaign managers and supporters are reduced to speculating about and arguing about what is important, but with little basis for assessing where the race stands, what issues are important, and what strategy they should follow to try to win a race. With information, a politician can formulate a plan.

Once a plan is created and implemented, polling allows candidates to track their success. Is name recognition increasing and is the candidate developing a positive image? Are attacks by the opponent having an effect and driving up negatives? Are attacks having an impact among specific groups, such that a counterattack is necessary? Are the voters who should be moving to support the candidate doing so? Are voters with specific issue concerns connecting with the candidate? The following pages will explain how campaigns use polling to achieve these objectives.

During all this, polling cannot provide issue positions for a candidate without any convictions. Campaigns begin with a candidate and the candidate's reasons for wanting to run for office. Candidates have to be able to offer voters a reason for electing them. The argument may be that he is better qualified, or that there are several important policy concerns that need to be addressed with a particular approach. Polling is then useful to decide how to present these concerns to the electorate. Polling is of limited use if the concern is to determine what the electorate cares about and then provide issue positions to a candidate without opinions. While many presume that "the tail wags the dog," campaigns that begin with that approach usually fail.

Note

1. Polls were showing that by May 2002, only 15 percent of voters, when asked an open-ended question about what should be the top priority for Congress, chose "Terrorism/fighting the war on terrorism" (Saad 2002).

Purposes, Limited Budgets, and When to Poll $\quad$ 2

O
NCE A CANDIDATE HAS DECIDED to poll, the next issue is when to poll. That depends on the amount of money a candidate has and the situation he faces. Polls are expensive, and the campaign budget usually determines how much polling can be done. Money is essential in two ways. Candidates have to have money to pay for polls. They also have to have enough money to be able to do something with the information. If a campaign is short of funds, it does no good to find that a particular constituency is not supporting the candidate and that it is necessary to get a message to that constituency. Polling is of limited value if information cannot be acted on.

Incumbents

Assuming the campaign has enough money, when to poll depends on the candidate and the situation he faces. Incumbents often poll well before a race. They need to know how the public perceives them after some time in office. Assuming they wish to run for reelection, they need to learn how well known they are, whether they are seen favorably, and how they are doing with particular groups. They need to know whether the public approves of how they are doing in office and what level of support they have for reelection. This information indicates whether they are vulnerable, and if so, on what issues and among which groups. The information can then serve as the basis for a plan of what the incumbent must do during the next year to reduce his vulnerability. To assess these possibilities, many incumbents poll a year or so prior to the election to learn which problems they need to address.

Challengers

Challengers face the sequential tasks of deciding whether to run and convincing others to support them. Polling can be done early (as much as six months to a year in advance) to respond to these two concerns.

First, the challenger may wish to assess her prospects of winning. She needs to check on her name recognition, the vulnerabilities of the incumbent, and the prospects of running a successful challenge. Campaigns are long, expensive, and demanding, and an initial investment in a poll provides some indication of the prospects of winning. If funds are limited, an initial poll to assess the situation can be very short, including little more than name recognition, reelection support, a matchup, and a few demographics. The goal is to find out very basic information to see if a race is winnable.

Second, challengers can use the results to convince the party to support them and to try to raise money. A challenger often faces the need to convince party officials that an incumbent can be beaten and that she is a viable candidate. Party officials will often require that a challenger pay for a poll to demonstrate there is a chance of winning before the party allocates resources to the challenger and asks others to offer support. If a challenger begins a race reasonably well known and a poll indicates that the incumbent is vulnerable, then the results can be presented to potential contributors to show them she is viable and to persuade them to donate. If the challenger is not well known, then the results from early polling may be so discouraging to supporters that they will not provide any assistance. If it is suspected this might be the case, then candidates generally campaign for a while and then poll, so their name recognition numbers will be higher.

Candidate Polling during Campaigns

Once a candidate enters a race, there is the difficult issue of when to acquire information. Again, polls are expensive, and few campaigns can poll as much as they want. The expense of polls compels campaigns to decide when to poll and which issues should be included.

Most campaigns, unless they have a very limited budget, begin with a benchmark poll, a poll that asks many questions about the candidates and issues and provides the information to establish a campaign plan. The content of such a poll will be discussed later.

The difficult decision is when to poll during a campaign. It is rare that a campaign can set specific times to poll in advance and stick with that schedule. Ideally, a campaign will establish a plan involving the presentation of issue positions at press conferences, door-to-door walks, direct mailings, and radio and television ads at particular times. The issue is when to poll to assess the effects of these activities and the actions of the opponent. If literature and ads are intended to increase the name recognition of the candidate, the issue is how long to wait to see what effect they are having. If the poll is done too soon, and there is little change, the results will discourage the candidate and campaign workers. Later in the campaign, the manager will need to assess the closeness of the race to determine whether more money should be spent and how it should be spent. If, for example, the candidate is weak in general, then it may be necessary to rely on blanket mailings, television ads, or radio. If the race is close, and the candidate is not doing well with Independent women (for example), then the campaign can respond with direct mail only to those voters.

The problem is that anticipating when information will be necessary is difficult. Contributions are often not as great as expected, or they do not occur when expected. A poll may be planned, but a budget shortfall may require postponing the poll. Then, there are events that are unanticipated. Negative stories appear about some past behavior of the candidate. The candidate says something inappropriate at a public forum. The opponent launches an unexpected ad attack, and there is concern that the ads are having a negative effect. In these situations, the campaign has to decide whether to deviate from the planned schedule of polling and conduct a poll to assess the current situation. Very often, politicians ask for a quick one-night poll after an incident which presents them negatively to see how many of the electorate followed the incident and their initial reaction to the incident. Did the issue harm the candidate's reputation? Is an ad seen as credible, and should the candidate respond?

In the 2002 New York gubernatorial election, someone leaked stories to the press about the Democratic candidate, Carl McCall, the comptroller, accusing him of writing letters to state officials asking them to look at resumes of friends for jobs. The campaign initially dismissed the likely damage from the news stories, but tracking polls quickly picked up that the stories were having a negative effect, so McCall researched the archives for all such stories and held a news conference in which he admitted to sixty-one such letters, in order to get past the incident. Quick polling made it possible to assess damage and to try to reduce its magnitude.

Campaigns also face a serious limit on how late during the race they can poll. While candidates may wish to poll as close to the election as possible to assess the impact of late campaign tactics, there is always the issue of polling early enough to allow sufficient time to use the information to respond. If polling is done too late, there is not enough time to create ads and buy television or radio time, or to send mail. The result of all these problems is that schedules of when to poll are always in flux during a campaign.

Party Organizations

Party organizations face two kinds of problems that may lead them to poll very early in a race. First, they may have competing candidates for a position, and they wish to avoid a primary that will cost the party lots of money and could lead the candidates to attack each other. A primary campaign with many negative attacks on each other by the candidates could produce a primary winner with much higher negatives (unfavorable ratings) and reduce the chances of the party's nominee succeeding in the general election. One way to avoid this is for the party leaders to commission a poll to test matchups for each candidate against the opponent from the other party. The party can then present these results to each candidate and ask the weaker one to drop out of the race and wait for another opportunity to run for office. A poll allows the party leaders to avoid the claim that they are arbitrarily favoring one candidate. If the results of the poll show one candidate stronger, they can be distributed to put pressure on the weaker one to drop out.

The other situation that party leaders face is how to allocate party money across several districts. The goal of a party is to win seats. Given limited campaign funds, they want to target the close races for which money is most needed and may have the greatest effect (Jacobson and Kernell 1983, 37; Jones and Borris 1985; Giles and Pritchard 1985; Stonecash 1988, 1994; Breaux and Gierzynski 1991; Gierzynski and Breaux 1991; Gierzynski 1992; Stonecash and Keith 1996). They want to spend the money they have on those candidates who have the best chance of winning. Party leaders first assess the candidates running and the strength of their opponents and classify districts as hopeless for the party, ones they might win, ones they are certain to win, and those that are uncertain as to outcome. The party will then commission polls in the districts that represent possibilities and those they cannot predict. These polls will usually be conducted six to eight months prior to the general election.

Party leaders take two approaches after getting these results. Sometimes they present the results to the candidates and tell them they will poll again two months prior to the election. Those with a good chance of winning and those who have significantly improved their situation will then receive party money. If the party has the money, it will conduct short tracking polls for the selected candidates with three to four weeks to go and then devote the remaining money to those in close races. In other cases the party leaders decide six to eight months prior to the election and decide at that point which races should get the bulk of the campaign funds. They will then poll during the two months prior to the election and decide whether they need to devote more money to some races and pull money from races that are likely to be lost or that their candidate is winning by a large margin.

The following is an example of a summary report to party leaders about candidate prospects in different county legislative districts. It is followed by another example, which is a summary of likely outcomes for U.S. Senate races that appeared unexpectedly during the summer of 2002.

Example 1: County Legislative Candidates: Name Recognition and Ratings

The following (see table 2.1) is an example of a poll done early in the campaign process. The poll was done in June of the year of the election. The information tells party leaders the relative name recognition and ratings for candidates for the November election. This poll was done for Republicans, trying to win control of the county legislature. All the Democrats were incumbents and the concern was whether it might be possible to beat any of them to gain seats.

Report Comments

The name recognition and ratings of existing Democratic incumbents are very diverse. Democrat 7 (63 percent favorable to 10 percent unfavorable), Democrat 9 (43 percent to 9 percent), and Democrat 22 (41 percent to 1 percent) are in a good position, while Democrat 14 (26 percent to 3 percent) and Democrat 24 (16 percent to 3 percent) do not begin in a good situation. All the challengers have low name recognition, except for Republican 7, who begins with good ratings (48 percent to 11 percent). Name recognition is a significant advantage in a low visibility race, and two of the Democratic incumbents (Democrat 9 and Democrat 22) begin with a major advantage over their challengers. Democrat 7, while he has a positive rating, does not hold an enormous advantage over Republican 7.

Table 2.1   Name Recognition and Ratings

District and Names	Favorable	Unfavorable	No Opinion	Never Heard Of
District 7				
Democrat	62.9	9.9	17.2	9.9
Republican	47.7	11.3	19.9	21.2
District 9				
Democrat	43.1	9.3	21.9	25.8
Republican	2.7	1.3	13.3	82.7
District 14				
Democrat	26.0	3.3	24.7	46.0
Republican	9.3	2.7	17.3	70.7
District 22				
Democrat	40.9	1.3	16.1	41.6
Republican	4.0	0.7	14.7	80.7
District 24				
Democrat	16.3	2.7	14.3	66.7
Republican	6.9	2.1	15.8	75.3

District Priorities: Recommendations

Drawing on all the prior information (presented earlier in the report)—district voting, enrollment, candidate ratings, reelection support, presence of self-defined conservatives, and self-reported voting for Republicans—I would suggest that the priorities for the campaign should be as follows.

PRIMARY EMPHASIS: DISTRICTS 7, 14, AND 24

In two of these districts (14 and 24), the incumbents have weak ratings, and the electoral conditions are generally favorable for a Republican to be elected. The challengers will have to work hard, but they begin against incumbents who are not in strong positions.

In district 7 the challenger begins in a good situation and the electoral conditions are favorable. The race will be difficult, however, because (the Democrat) begins with very good ratings. We asked if, now that (the Democrat) is seventy years old, it was time for someone new, or his age is not an issue. About 27 percent said it is time for someone new, but 65 percent said it is not an issue. Those who think it is time for someone new are very negative about his reelection (23 percent reelect to 65 percent someone new) while those who do not think it is an issue are very supportive (51 percent reelect to 21 percent someone new). Making an issue out of (the Democrat's) age will hurt more than it will help. In district 14, there is considerable opposition to building a third runway (at the local airport, near a suburban housing area). About 31 percent favor this, and 49 percent oppose it. This opposition is uniform across party groups.

These three districts are the ones that should receive the primary attention during the campaign.

SECONDARY EMPHASIS: DISTRICTS 9 AND 22

In these districts the incumbents have good ratings, good reelection support, and the electoral conditions are less favorable for a Republican to get elected. The challengers are also not well known. These are districts where the challenger will have to make a significant effort—largely through door-to-door—to build some name recognition. We can provide them with lists of likely voters and then repoll them in early September to assess how successful the candidates have been in creating name recognition. If they have been successful, these campaigns could receive more funding.

Note on the Outcome

Following this initial poll, the county leaders told candidates they would poll again in early September to see who had made substantial progress in building name recognition. That polling resulted in two districts being dropped from further consideration. A poll was then conducted in mid-October, and considerable party money was devoted to three of the races. Republicans eventually won districts 14 and 24 in close elections.

Example 2: White House Assessments of Senate Races, June 2002

The same kinds of assessments occur at the national level. In June 2002, a White House intern, on the way to a presentation to be made to Republicans by presidential advisor Karl Rove, dropped a computer disk containing the presentation in Lafayette Park. A Senate Democratic staffer picked it up and got it to the *New York Times,* which mounted it on its web page.[1] The presentation included a map, presented below, assessing the prospects for winning specific seats.

When parties make these assessments, they are very concerned about keeping them secret. The publication of this map indicates the problems that can follow when such information is released. If the party indicates that they think a specific candidate may lose, it can have several effects, and one of them can be very bad for their candidate. The suggestion that a race is going to be close may mobilize party supporters, contributors, and workers to do more to try to keep a candidate. But the release may also harm their candidate. The prediction that a candidate may lose may discourage contributors and make it more difficult to raise the money necessary for a close race. It may also encourage contributors who were trying to decide whether to donate to the opponent. This will make the race even more difficult. The report suggested that Tim Hutchinson, the incumbent senator from Arkansas, was vulnerable and could lose. After the report became public, the White House aide spent the rest of the day trying to assure everyone that Senator Hutchinson was "in a strong position to win re-election" (Bumiller 2002, A28).

Figure 2.1

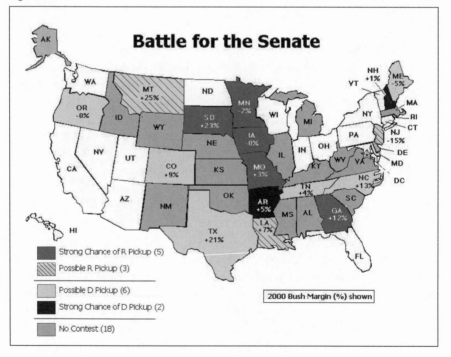

Note

1. As of the summer of 2002, the entire report could be downloaded from www.nytimes.com/auth/login?URI = http://www.nytimes.com/2002/06/14/politics/14ROVE.html.

What Kind of Poll?   3

Testing the Waters: Initial Matchups

CANDIDATES GENERALLY CONDUCT three kinds of polls during campaigns. As noted before, many candidates, largely challengers, do a short poll before officially getting into a race to decide whether they have a chance of winning. In these cases, the poll usually includes a limited number of questions, focusing on name recognition and ratings and the matchup. A few issues might be included, but the emphasis is primarily on levels of name recognition for a candidate and the opponent, job approval for an incumbent, support for reelection of an incumbent, and an early matchup.

While candidates hope the results will make it clear what they should do, there are always issues of interpretation and ambition involved. Table 3.1 provides examples of three different situations that candidates can face. The first involves a case in which the information was very clear. A Democratic challenger was running versus a well-established Republican officeholder. The Democrat in this case had already decided to enter the race, but this August poll indicated that the challenger had little chance to make a race of it. When faced with such results, most candidates either drop out or make a minimal effort to campaign.

Table 3.1 Initial Matchups

	Republican	Democrat	No Choice
Incumbent R—Challenger D	72.3	15.3	12.4
Incumbent R—Incumbent D	26.5	46.3	27.2

	Candidate 1	Candidate 2	No Choice
Open Seat R—Open Seat R	5.3	18.9	75.8

In other cases, the results are less definitive. The second matchup involved two incumbents thrown into a new district against each other because of reapportionment. In this case, both intended to stay in the race, so the early poll was just to indicate the challenge faced by the incumbent Republican, who had been in office only one year. The poll indicated that the Republican candidate was losing by a large margin to the Democrat. The Republican was not as well known as the Democrat, and it was unclear if she could overcome the name recognition disadvantage. As is always the case with these early polls, there is an effort to assess whether the bad news is offset by other more encouraging information. In this case, much of the new district was new territory for both candidates, so there were reasons to believe that the Republican could do as well in these areas as the Democrat. The Democrat, after a number of years in office, was not able to get over 50 percent in the matchup, indicating some weaknesses. But the Republican, being less well known, also had problems. She was not well known by Republicans, and her party was choosing her in the matchup at a rate less than Democrats were choosing the Democratic candidate. The Republican, assuming that she could mobilize her own party by November, did not see the results as very discouraging. The political context is important in assessing results.

The last situation involves even greater uncertainty. In another open seat, two candidates were vying for the party nomination. Candidate 2 was designated as the party nominee at a meeting of party committee members. Candidate 1, with almost no name recognition, was faced with results that indicated only 5 percent of likely voters supported him. The results were not entirely discouraging, however, because the results indicated that candidate 2, after more than a decade in local offices, was also not very well known. Approximately 75 percent of likely voters had not made a choice, so there was not a problem of converting voters who had made a decision. Candidate 1 took the results as a sign that his opponent was not that strong and that the race was winnable. Since this was one of the few open seats to occur in the area, he began a primary race.

Benchmarks and Campaign Plans

Once a candidate has definitely decided to enter a race, assuming she has raised sufficient funds, the next step is to conduct a "benchmark" poll. This is a poll that asks questions about numerous issues so the campaign can establish a plan. Benchmark polls provide extensive information on voter views of the candidates, the distribution of opinion on current issues, and the connection of issues to current voter inclinations. These surveys are generally four to nine pages in length and cover many issues, some of which may eventually prove to be irrelevant to the campaign.

The process of conducting a benchmark poll begins with a meeting with the candidate, the campaign manager, and the pollster. This first meeting often provides an indication of whether the candidate is ready for a campaign. Candidates who hope to win need to offer voters a reason for electing them. Campaigns are easier to plan when a candidate can offer his sense of the important issues and the themes he wishes to emphasize. While polling is very valuable to help a candidate sort out what themes to present, it is a sign of trouble when a candidate does not have issues he cares about and can present articulately and with some passion. Some candidates cannot offer a reason for why they want to be elected, other than that they have waited for this opportunity. These individuals often arrive at this meeting and ask the pollster what issues they should discuss. They are candidates with a goal but without a reason for the goal to offer the electorate.

When an initial meeting occurs, it is important to obtain a full sense of the issues that might play a role during the campaign. The following questions should be asked.

Questions for the Candidate and Campaign

- What are the important issues within the political jurisdiction? For each issue, what is the background on the issue and what are the alternatives that may play out during the campaign? One of the most important matters is to boil the issues down to some relatively simple alternative positions that can be explained and presented to voters in a survey script.
- What are the primary themes the candidate will push during the campaign? What themes will the opponent be likely to present? What are the issues upon which the two disagree and on which do they agree? Is there a sense that some issues are likely to be more important than others?
- What background does the candidate have that will be valuable to stress, and what background will be detrimental? It is important to ask the candidate about any past problems so their effect

can be gauged. The important matter is to assess the vulnerabilities of each candidate who may emerge during the campaign.

- What demographics (income, recent economic situation, education, marital status, union membership, working status) should be asked about, and what questions about personal views (self-defined ideology, abortion, or gun control) are important to include?

Tracking Polls

Finally, as the campaign proceeds, tracking polls are done (table 3.2). These are surveys with fewer questions, focusing on the candidates and only those issues deemed crucial for the campaign. They are used to assess the progress of the campaign. Is name recognition rising, and how are the images of the candidates evolving? How close is the election matchup, and what issues are playing a major role in affecting choices? Costs are again a crucial issue here. Campaigns may like to track once a week, but that is expensive. Campaigns that realize they have a close contest and have sufficient resources may decide to poll once a week to see how the race is evolving. In some cases these tracking polls can create very tense situations. If a race is close with two weeks to go, candidates often face the difficult decision of whether to borrow money for last-minute ads.[1]

Table 3.2   Reelection Support

Q 3. Do you think (Democrat) should be reelected or is it time to give someone new a chance?

	5/99	7/99	9/99 I	9/99 II	10/99	10/99 II
Reelect	37.9	46.0	49.2	50.8	51.7	48.0
Someone new	39.3	34.1	31.2	32.0	32.0	28.3
No opinion	22.9	19.8	19.6	17.2	16.3	22.7

Example: Tracking an Election

Tracking polls indicate how a race is evolving. Figure 3.1 shows the favorable and unfavorable ratings of two mayoral candidates. The Democratic incumbent, first elected in 1995, had gradually improved her ratings from 1996 through early 1999, the year of her reelection bid. The concern of the campaign was how the situation of the Republican challenger was evolving. By July of 1999 his favorable ratings had improved, and his negatives were at about the same level as the Democrat's. Further, as shown below, the reelection percentage for the incumbent Democrat was not over 50 percent, a sign of weak support.

Faced with this situation, the Democrat decided it was time to increase her criticism of the challenger. She launched a series of ads criticizing some of his past votes on the City Council. The result was that it drove his negatives up, reduced his percentage in the matchup, and the Democrat was able to win a relatively close race. The tracking polls were crucial to indicate the need to alter strategy and increase the criticism of the opponent.

Figure 3.1 Democrat and Republican Mayoral Candidate Ratings, 1996–1999

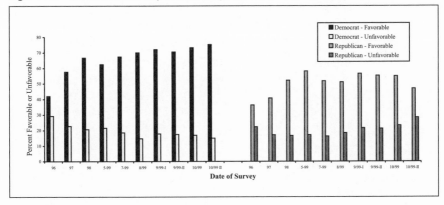

Note

1. In one race I worked a poll ten days prior to the election that showed the race dead even. The Democrat then borrowed and spent $30,000. He went to bed at 1:00 in the morning assuming he had lost the race by one hundred votes. At 3:30 in the morning, his staff woke him up to tell him he won by thirty-three votes. The last-minute polling was crucial.

Writing Questions: Language and the Script 4

Hiring a Pollster

THE FIRST STEP IN POLLING is to hire a pollster. There are several things to look for in a pollster. First, select someone who has experience conducting polls. Everyone must start somewhere, but a campaign can be lost if someone is doing his first poll and makes mistakes. If a person has experience, it is valuable to ask for references and ask about the quality of work done, including being timely, writing good reports, and being able to work with people with different opinions during the campaign. Second, have a discussion with the pollster about how the process will proceed. A pollster should be able to explain how he proceeds, the process of writing a script, his understanding of the importance of the candidate signing off, how he draws samples and from what lists, and how long the entire process should take. Make sure the cost is known before beginning. Third, if possible, find someone from the area. That individual will know what the local issues are and how much attention they have received. The campaign will have to spend less time explaining the issues. Fourth, hire someone who listens and focuses on your campaign and who does not try to use scripts from other campaigns. Candidates spend a lot of time talking with people, and they are very aware of what issues are discussed and what language is used to discuss the issues. It is important to have someone who listens to the candidate and campaign staff and incorporates their ideas, if not always their language. Finally, as in any endeavor in which there must be a lot of discussion and exchange, it is important to work with someone you feel you can get along with.

The Process of Writing a Script

After an initial meeting to discuss the possible issues of the campaign, the next step is to write the script for the survey. The script is crucial as the mechanism for gathering information. It must ask about the right issues, with the right language and alternatives, and with questions in the right sequence. It provides general instructions for callers and the specific language that callers must use while questioning respondents. This language must be precise.

The process of writing the script is very important. A survey script should be written by one person, but it should be reviewed by the candidate and the significant campaign workers. It is not uncommon for a script to go through three to four drafts before approval. This review process is very valuable. Those who work in politics and campaigns are knowledgeable about how issues are seen, and their perspective is essential to make sure that the language used approximates the language that those involved in politics are hearing.

The review process is also important to avoid resistance to the results once a report is delivered. Candidates often do not like the results. They often like to believe the (bad) result is a consequence of the way a question is worded. The best way to avoid this problem is to work closely with the candidate and the campaign manager to get their agreement to the language in questions before the survey is conducted.

The process of arriving at a script is for a pollster to write a first draft and then hold a small meeting (three to six people) to review the language. It is valuable to have everyone present at once so differences of opinion can be aired. This allows an exchange of views, and hopefully a consensus will emerge about what are likely to be the important issues and what language should be used. After this meeting the pollster writes another draft and circulates it. If there is not extensive disagreement, the discussions about editing can be one-on-one. If there are significant disagreements, another meeting should take place. Editing continues until the candidate and campaign managers are satisfied. This process can be lengthy, but it is important to make sure that the candidate and campaign manager are confident that the questions asked and the language used are appropriate. If they are not, they are more likely to be skeptical of results they don't like and less likely to listen to the advice delivered. Then money and time have been lost, and there will be tensions between the pollster and the campaign.

It is important in the early stages of writing a script to establish the importance of seeking objective information. It does the campaign no good to include information that portrays the client in only a positive light and the opponent in only negative terms. During a campaign both sides will present positive and negative information, and it is crucial to make sure that the polling process probes for the effect of the information most likely to emerge during the campaign. This can help the campaign anticipate problems that may emerge later. The job of a pollster is to help the candidate. It is important not to allow questions to be asked in ways that just reassure the candidate.

Content and Sequence

Surveys have a fairly standard format. They usually begin with one or more general lead-in questions, followed by questions about name recognition, job approval, reelection support, and the matchup. The questions about specific issues are asked. The survey usually ends with demographic questions. A sample survey is included at the end of the book.

The general lead-in questions are designed to elicit general assessments of the area. A common one is: "Do you think things in the (neighborhood, city, state, nation) are headed in the right direction or the wrong direction?" This kind of question is very valuable to pick up on optimism or pessimism. The question also makes it possible to see if those in either category (optimists and pessimists) are supportive of or opposed to an incumbent. Incumbents worry that if the local economy is not doing well, the electorate will hold them accountable and support any challenger against them. This kind of question makes it possible to assess such a possibility.

This question is usually followed by one about name recognition and ratings of individuals. Many candidates are not well known. Most voters do not follow politics closely. Presidential elections receive the most attention, and even those are not followed closely by everyone (Patterson 2002). State and local politics receive even less press coverage and less attention from voters. The major problem most candidates face is becoming known by the electorate. The question about name recognition provides crucial information about the visibility and ratings of the candidate. This question should come very early so it captures voter reactions without introducing any other information. The goal is to assess how well voters know candidates without providing any promptings of information. An example of this is shown in table 4.1. The specific alternatives provided make it possible to determine overall name recognition (100 percent minus the percentage of those who have never heard of the candidate) and the rating of the candidate (the ratio of favorable to unfavorable ratings). The no-opinion category indicates those who have heard of the candidate but have no clear impression of her.

If possible, it is better to include a number of politicians in addition to the specific candidates in the race to be polled. It makes it a little less obvious who the poll might be for. Respondents will figure that out if a matchup is included, but sometimes more than one matchup will be included if the race is citywide or countywide. Including other politicians is also valuable because the candidate can then call the others and share the information with them as a favor. Doing that favor creates a slight indebtedness and the favor may be returned by the other official at a later date.

Table 4.1   Question on Name Recognition and Ratings

Q. Next I'd like to read you the names of some people who have been in the news recently. For each name, could you please tell me whether your impressions of that person are favorable or unfavorable. If you have never heard of someone, or don't know enough to rate the person, just say so.

	Favorable	Unfavorable	No Opinion	Never Heard Of
Candidate 1	1	2	3	4
Candidate 2	1	2	3	4
Candidate 3	1	2	3	4
Candidate 4	1	2	3	4
Candidate 5	1	2	3	4

The name recognition question is usually followed by questions about job approval, support for reelection, and the matchup (table 4.2). If an incumbent conducts a poll before a challenger is known, the first two can still be asked to indicate the incumbent's level of support in the electorate. With these questions, the goal is to determine if the incumbent is seen positively, or if there are problems. The goal is not to test for whether voters know who holds a specific office, but to determine reactions to an incumbent now in office, so information on the office held should be provided to voters.

Table 4.2   Job Approval and Reelection

Q. Do you approve or disapprove of the job (incumbent) is doing as county executive?

    1 ____ approve   2 ____ disapprove   3 ____ no opinion

Q. This November there will be an election for the office of _____. Do you think (incumbent) should be reelected, or is it time to give someone else a chance to do better?

    1 ____ reelect   2 ____ someone new   3 ____ no opinion

These questions should be asked early in the poll, before questions are presented about issues, controversies, or scandals that may have occurred while the incumbent has been in office. The goal is to obtain a general reaction from voters without reminding them of either positive or negative information that might affect this general judgment. If voters are reminded of many policy problems or issues in the jurisdiction and then asked for their general job approval, approval ratings will probably be lower (Benton and Daly 1991). Information about these matters may or may not emerge during the campaign, and voters may or may not absorb that information. The goal of asking the question early is to determine the most general reaction without the influence of information, so the question should come in the beginning.

The general principle of surveys, which should be applied in deciding the overall sequence of questions, is to not introduce any information prior to a question that could influence the responses to that question. It is not appropriate to ask how the mayor is handling city finances after a question that tells voters the city has a large budget deficit and then asks about what solutions should be used. This attention to sequence requires considerable thought, and any survey should be reviewed after all language editing is completed to see if there are sequence issues. Questions that push respondents to make choices on issues (to be discussed later) should go toward the end of the survey.

Following the questions about reelection and job approval, if a challenger is known, then the matchup question can be asked. In asking this question, the goal is to provide the respondent with the same information she will be presented with in the voting booth. Many voters make their choice based on the party of the candidate, so respondents should be provided with that information. An example of such a question is presented below (table 4.3). These questions about the incumbent and the matchup are then followed by questions about issues and demographics.

Table 4.3   The Matchup

Q. This November in the election for mayor, the candidates will be _____, the Democrat, and _____, the Republican. Would you most likely vote for (Democrat) or (Republican)?

    1 ___ (Democrat)   2 ___ (Republican)   3 ___ no opinion

The "No Opinion" Issue

In asking these questions about job approval, reelection support, and the matchup, and with all other questions, there is the issue of how to handle the "no opinion" option. Every time a question is asked, there is the option of explicitly presenting the respondent with the option of "no opinion" or omitting it and making him volunteer it. The former makes it clear to the respondent that the option of no opinion is a very appropriate response, while the latter "pushes" the respondent to make a choice.[1] This involves a central issue in public opinion surveys: do many voters really have no opinion (Converse 1964, 1970; Schuman and Presser 1981, 147–60; Asher 1992, 21–37), or do they have latent opinions, which they may be reluctant to express and should be pushed to reveal these opinions under the presumption that they just need to be prompted (Sanchez and Morchio 1992; Gilljam and Granberg 1993; Blais, et al. 2000). If the option is made explicit, the percentage choosing it will be higher, so the issue must be dealt with.

There are arguments for each approach, and these arguments are particularly important when asking about job approval, reelection support, and vote choice in a matchup. The advocates of not offering the option argue that voters are likely to lean one way or the other and by the end of the campaign the "leaners" will eventually end up at the "pushed" position, so you might as well find out that likely position and the eventual degree of support when you contact the individual. On the other hand, the support for a candidate may be relatively soft, and it is crucial to know about that soft support early in the campaign to have a realistic view of the candidate's position. This is particularly important when a candidate has not been in office very long and it is likely that the public does not really know what a candidate has done. It is valuable for the campaign manager to know if awareness of the candidate is not as high as it might seem. It is also valuable, if many people are unaware of an incumbent's record, for a campaign manager to put that information in front of an incumbent to make him work harder. An incumbent can have relatively high name recognition, and his image may be positive. The electorate may not, however, know much about what the official has actually done. Their vague impression is positive, but without much depth or content. To assess that, it is better to offer the option of "or don't you know enough to judge that?" The issue of whether to probe for ignorance or push respondents is something that must be discussed at the beginning of the process.

Probing for Intensity

There is also the issue of whether to try to gauge degrees of support. Voters may support reelection or choose the candidate in a matchup, but support may be weak or "soft." If so, the candidate has to worry about support evaporating in the face of attack ads. To assess degrees of support, a question should be asked and then followed up with a probe for strength of feeling. For job approval, the follow-up would be "is that strongly or just approve?" or "is that strongly or just disapprove?" For reelection support and vote choice, the follow-up would be "would that be definitely or just reelect _____?" or "would that be definitely or just elect someone new?" For the matchup question, two probes might occur. If a choice is made, a "definitely or probably" follow-up can occur. If a respondent says "no choice," then those who choose no choice are presented with the question "Would you lean to either _____ or _____?" Those making a choice in the second question are then coded as having a choice. This approach provides a portrait of the distribution of support and allows a comparison of the relative strength of support for the two candidates. If the matchup question is also added with the "definitely or just" probe, then it is possible to compare support from "definitely" to "probably" to "lean" for each candidate.

While including all these probes might seem to be the obvious choice for a survey, it does involve asking more questions. Rather than three quick questions about job approval, reelection, and the match-up, the questioning can become six questions (each question plus a probe). This may seem trivial, but this consumes more time and increases the length of the survey. Each decision to probe for more information has that effect and can run up the cost of the survey or require cutting out some issue questions.

Issue Questions: Purpose, Content, and Language

The goal of conducting political polls is to get accurate information. Despite all the negative stories about polling as a manipulative process, the primary concern with polling is to ask questions in a way that mini-mizes bias and produces accurate results. Bias refers to producing responses that are different from the views people actually hold. To get accurate results, make sure that the questions are not the source of those biased results. It does no good to pay thousands of dollars for a survey that provides misleading results. Biased results damage the campaign. They also harm the reputation of the specific pollster. If a campaign trusts results that are a product of biased questions and the candidate loses, the pollster will eventually receive less business and will find her career in jeopardy. It is essential to present accurate results, no matter how much they are disliked and treated skeptically by the candidate.[2] To obtain unbiased responses, a number of rules of question writing are important.

Clarity of Purpose

The first matter to address when writing issue questions is what infor-mation is desired. Even before a poll is conducted, a candidate and a campaign manager should have discussed what they think will be the major issues during the campaign. They should have a good idea of how these issues will be discussed—what language will be used and what alternatives will be relevant for the campaign. They should have a good idea of the way they want to present the candidate and how they want to contrast her with the opponent. They should have thought about the contrast the opponent will try to make. These pre-liminary discussions provide the basis for deciding what questions to ask and how to ask them. What are the issues and exactly what infor-mation is desired from each question?

The next step is to try to get precise about the information goals. Very often candidates or campaign managers will casually run through a set of issues they want to ask about and assume they can leave the problem of the specific language to the pollster. It is important to slow them down and discuss the issue to know just what they want to find out about it. Do they want to know what people see as the alternatives, how people choose between two alternative solutions that are emerging from public discussions, which candidate people think is most capable of resolving or handling the issue, or even whether people see this as an issue that has a solution? There should be thorough discussions about what information is desired and how it will be useful to the campaign.

If information cannot or will not be used, there is probably little use in gathering it. A candidate or a campaign might be curious about some issue but have no idea how to use it or have specifically decided not to use it. With regard to the former, a lawsuit may have been lost by the city, county, or state about the treatment of an individual. The candidate may want to see if the issue registers with voters and whether the outcome is accepted. If the candidate is not willing to use the issue during the campaign, there is little use in pursing the information.[3] In other situations, the candidate may be aware of some personal problem of the opponent but be unwilling to use it in a campaign.[4]

Language

The language of questions should be simple and direct. It is essential to use language that the average person can understand. If there is any ambiguity to terms (they may mean different things to different respondents), then the language should be revised to make sure the meaning is clear (Fowler 1992). The essential logic of surveys is to present each respondent with a clear statement of an issue so that each respondent has the same sense of what is being asked about. To take a simple example, a survey might ask "Do you think that Social Security obligations present a serious problem for the federal budget?" with the implied alternatives of *yes* or *no*. The difficulty is that one respondent may answer *yes*, but mean that Social Security is consuming too much of the budget and should be constrained. Another respondent may be operating from a view that more should be set aside to support this commitment, and *yes* may mean that more of the budget should be set aside. The language needs revision. Before doing this, as noted above, the first matter is to discuss why the question is being asked and what information is desired. If the concern is to pull out reactions about the relative devotion of budget resources to Social Security, the question might be "With regard to the federal budget and support of Social Security, do you think not enough is being allocated to support this, about the right amount, or is not enough being allocated to support this?" If the goal is to see if there are anxieties about future funding for Social Security (which an opponent might exploit), the question might be "With regard to the future of Social Security, do you worry that there will not be enough money for Social Security in the future, or do you think Congress will find enough money in the future?"

If an issue is usually discussed in complex language by experts or government officials, some way has to be found to express it in everyday language. Questions should also be as short as possible. It is difficult for respondents to follow long questions. It is difficult for callers to read long sentences and long questions. Just as with other writing, it is important to write the script several days prior to conducting the survey and then to return to the script several times to edit it to reduce the amount of language the respondent hears on the telephone. Respondents will be more attentive if questions are shorter and more likely to stay engaged.

Simplify and Separate Issues

If an issue is complicated, it is necessary to simplify it to the essential issues involved so it can be presented to respondents. If an issue involves multiple concerns, it is best to break it up into a series of separate questions. Each question should ask about only one concern. This way it will be clear what an answer is in response to. The abortion issue provides an example. There is the issue of whether abortion should be allowed. There is also the question of whether state governments should be allowed to use Medicaid funding to pay for abortions. It is not appropriate to ask "Should abortion be allowed and abortions paid for with government funds?" These are two questions packed into one question, and it would not be clear whether a response is about abortion or government funding. This should be broken up into two questions such as the following (table 4.4).

Table 4.4   The Abortion Issue

Q. On the abortion issue, do you regard yourself as pro-choice or pro-life?

    1 ___ pro-choice   2 ___ pro-life   3 ___ no opinion

Q. Do you favor or oppose the use of government funds to pay for abortion for low-income individuals?

    1 ___ favor   2 ___ oppose   3 ___ no opinion

As another example, during the 2000 elections the proposal to create separate Social Security accounts for individuals became an issue. The issue involved two questions: whether individual accounts should be created and who should manage them. It would not be appropriate to ask "Do you favor or oppose the creation of individual Social Security accounts managed by private companies?" Breaking this into "Should there be individual accounts?" and "Who should manage them?" allows respondents to provide specific responses to different issues and provides the candidate with more detailed information about public opinion (table 4.5).

Table 4.5   Social Security

Q. There is a proposal to take some of the surplus and create individual investment accounts for retirement. The accounts would not replace Social Security, but would add to those benefits in years when there is a surplus. Would you support or oppose this proposal?

    1 ___ support   2 ___ oppose   3 ___ no opinion

Q. If such accounts were established, would you prefer that government manage the investments, or let individuals do it on their own?

    1 ___ government   2 ___ individuals   3 ___ no opinion

Provide Alternatives

The logic of polling is to provide all respondents with the same stimuli and then assess the responses. To make sure that all respondents get the same alternatives, each question should include the alternatives to be considered. If the question does not present the respondent with alternatives, there is no way to know that x percent of respondents in a specific category chose alternative y relative to x and z when confronted with a question. To make sure all respondents are aware of the choices and all get the same set of choices, the alternatives should be read to the respondent at the end of the question. For example, it is ambiguous to ask "Where do you stand on the issue of abortion?" With this way of presenting the question, the respondent may have a different sense of the relevant options than the pollster. If the desired choices are "pro-choice" and "pro-life," those alternatives should be presented.

Provide Alternatives That Are Meaningful and Legitimate

If alternatives are to be presented, it is crucial to make sure that they are meaningful and realistic. Questions about taxes present an example of this. Often candidates want to ask the question "Are your taxes too high?" This question has two problems. First, few people will ever say their taxes are too low, so this is not a meaningful alternative. It does not represent an alternative people will be thinking about. Second, while the *yes* and *no* responses might be interesting, the alternatives of *yes* and *no* probably do not represent the real issues involved. The usual issue is whether taxes are too high, given the services provided. Some may simply dislike the level of taxation. Others may think there are too many services provided. Others may perceive that there is a lot of waste or inefficiency. The newspapers might have been filled with stories of too many workers on government payrolls. A relatively simple alternative is to ask "Do you think your taxes are too high for the services provided, about right, or low for what you get?" If taxes and services are likely to be a major issue in a campaign, then the question needs to be worked over carefully to allow various opinions to be expressed. Another alternative is to present respondents with several choices and ask which best describes their view. The following example (table 4.6) is an attempt to give respondents more choices.

School vouchers are another example of an issue that could be presented simply or with some complexity. The question might be relatively simple, as in the first option in table 4.7. Another method is to frame the question in the way politicians on each side are trying to frame the issue. In this case, the judgment is that the primary alternative positions are whether people see vouchers as providing opportunity or undermining schools. The issue could also be framed as a

Table 4.6   Local Taxes and Services

Q. Which of the following best describes your views about local taxes and services?

1 ___ Taxes are too high and government provides too many services

2 ___ Services are about right, but there is too much waste and inefficiency, resulting in taxes that are too high for what we get

3 ___ Services and taxes are about right

4 ___ Services are not adequate, and I would be willing to pay more to get the services

5 ___ No opinion

---

way of holding public schools accountable. In trying to decide how to ask the question, one criterion should be the way the debate over the issue is developing. But the way the candidate wants to talk about the issue also has to play a role. The challenge is to find wording that allows both goals to be achieved. If that cannot be done and the issue is important, then multiple questions will be necessary.

Table 4.7   School Vouchers

Q. Do you support or oppose vouchers, or a grant of a set amount from local school budgets, for students to go wherever they wish?

1 ___ support   2 ___ oppose   3 ___ no opinion

Q. Vouchers—grants of money to students to attend other schools—have been proposed for poorer students. Do you see vouchers as an opportunity for the poor to receive an education like the more affluent have or do you see vouchers as undermining public schools?

1 ___ opportunity   2 ___ undermining   3 ___ both

4 ___ no opinion

Alternatives must also be legitimate. The goal is to get those with differing views to express them. Alternatives must be expressed in language that communicates the concerns of those with differing views and presents the choices as reasonable and respectable.[5] If one alternative is presented in a negative way, fewer respondents will select it, even though they may support the position, and the results will be biased. To return to the abortion issue, it is not appropriate to use a question such as "Do you support a policy that allows killing fetuses or do you respect the sanctity of life?" For those who are squeamish about what abortion involves but support the right of women to make their own choices, the language of the first alternative will inhibit them from selecting that option and underrepresent the percentage that supports the right of women to have abortions. A more appropriate way to present the alternatives might be "Are you more concerned about the right of women to make their own choices or about protecting fetuses?" Again, the goal is to draw out different positions and make those positions legitimate and respectable alternatives, so the language must reflect those differences.

As another example, a candidate might want to know how people feel about providing more aid to local schools. The question "Do you support or oppose providing significant increases in aid to local schools?" could be asked. As simple as the question may seem, it has problems. It may be difficult for some respondents, who are proeducation but worried about taxes and the effectiveness of schools, to indicate they do not want to support the schools. The option of *no* sounds antischool and for some is not an appealing alternative to choose. It does not reflect their position. The question does not provide alternatives for those with doubts about the effectiveness of schools, and the alternatives have to present that language so a respondent feels comfortable choosing it. The first question in table 4.8 is one way to simplify this issue and present two broad alternatives so that those who believe in spending and those who believe in standards can express their views. The second question allows for more diversity of views, which could be important to capture if schools and funding are likely to be important during the campaign. Again, it is important to listen carefully to the candidate. She may really not want to focus on these alternatives but may be willing to vote for more school aid (and the necessary taxes), if administrative costs are lowered. The polling then has to assess how much people see that as a problem and if they find her position appealing.

Table 4.8   Improving Schools

Q. There is a lot of discussion about improving schools. Do you think the best way to improve schools is to provide more money to hire better teachers and build better schools, or is it to work with existing funds and set higher standards for students and teachers? (*Do not offer both, but record if offered.*)

    1 ___ spend more 2 ___ standards 3___ both 4 ___ no opinion

Q. Many candidates for mayor are talking about the need to improve education in the city public schools. If you were mayor, which of the following would be your first priority? (*Read list.*)

    1 ___ Spend more money to hire more teachers
    2 ___ Spend more money to rebuild city schools
    3 ___ Improve student discipline
    4 ___ Set higher academic standards for students
    5 ___ Set higher standards for teachers
    6 ___ Other (*Do not read, but record.*)

Again, the goal of a survey is to draw out differences of opinion that exist within a political jurisdiction. The intent is to make sure the extent of difference is known and to know how people with different views are likely to vote. To make sure that questions present these differences, it is important that a survey be written in consultation with those who are aware of the issues and know the language that is used by people with differing opinions. It is also important to show the language to others, get their reaction, and edit questions in response to suggestions that the language does not quite capture the alternatives. To repeat, editing and revising a script are very important. How questions are asked affects results (Martin and Polivka 1995).

"Push" Polling and "Push" Questions

To many people, the most negative aspect of polling involves "push" polling. This practice is widely characterized as unethical, manipulative of respondents, and contributing to the distortion of political campaigns. While the term push polling has a general negative connotation in the press, it is important to clearly distinguish two different ways in which the term "push" is used. Push polling is very infrequently used, but achieves considerable notoriety when it is used. Push questions, on the other hand, are widely used, but not in the way that many assume.

First, what is push polling? This notorious practice involves a caller presenting a respondent with explicitly negative information about a candidate and then asking if the information makes the respondent more or less likely to vote for the candidate. In many cases the information presented to the respondent is not true. For example, a campaign might call and ask "Does the fact that _____ has had problems with the IRS make you more or less likely to vote for her?" Or, to plant rumors about the character of the candidate, the survey might say "Does the fact that the police have been called to the home of _____ because of problems of spouse abuse make you more or less likely to vote for him?" The questions present information as factual, when the goal may be to begin a rumor about a candidate that will hurt his chances of winning an election. Critics of polling often point to this practice as an indication that polling undermines the democratic process by serving as a mechanism to plant lies about candidates, under the guise of conducting a poll.

While this might be seen as a common tactic, it is used very infrequently because it generally causes serious problems for the campaign using this approach. If a candidate authorizes a poll with such questions, or a supporter conducts a phone bank using this approach, the sequence of events that follows such activities is fairly predictable. The calling process will invariably contact an individual who is a partisan supporter of the candidate mentioned. The respondent will doubt the "fact" or be angered by the use of such a statement in a purported poll, and will then call the media. Reporters, who thrive on exposing political chicanery, will interview the respondent and write a story about one of the candidates using "dirty tactics." The result will be several days of negative headlines for the campaign of the candidate making the calls.[6] The campaign will have to deny that it made the calls, which may prompt more investigative reporting and more embarrassing stories about the approach the campaign is taking. The alternative is to apologize, which will also not do the campaign any good. An apology will give the impression that the campaign did engage in the activity, which will do further harm. The lack of an apology will also hurt, of course, because it will give the appearance of being uncaring. There is much to lose in employing this tactic.

This scenario emerged in the 2000 presidential election. Early in the Republican primary, stories emerged that calls made by the Bush campaign to likely Republican voters in South Carolina involved disparaging language about opponent John McCain. McCain was able to portray himself as the victim of unfair practices, while Bush was forced to disavow the practice. While it is not clear just what was said and how much the Bush campaign was behind whatever was said, the result was several days of negative headlines about the tactics of the Bush campaign.[7] George Bush disassociated his campaign and denounced the practice, and was able to move on to win the nomination.

The worse forms of push polling almost always create more problems than benefits. Even if push polling is done under the presumption that the results can be used as legitimate polling results, the information derived from presenting a false statement will be of no use in a campaign. If a negative and completely inaccurate statement is presented to respondents, it will invariably make people less likely to vote for a candidate. The problem is that there is generally nothing the campaign can do with the information, unless they are willing to present inaccurate information right at the end of the campaign, when there is limited time to respond. Most campaigns are not willing to do this, and those that might consider it are hesitant because of the ability of the media to expose the tactic within the last two to three days of the campaign, leaving the instigating campaign no time to recover. It could be more trouble than it is worth for a campaign. In sum, while the practice of planting negative information is presumed to exist, there are powerful reasons not to do it, and only a few candidates engage in this practice.

While campaigns do not use surveys to plant false information, they do conduct polls that use questions that present negative information about candidates to get voter reactions to gauge the effect of the information. This involves a set of push questions. The term push is used to mean that specific negative and positive information is presented and the goal is to see if the information pushes the evaluation of the candidate.

Campaigns usually have positive and negative information about their candidate and about the opponent. The difficult issue is what to do with all this information. Budget limits make it impossible to tell voters all the positive things a candidate has done and all the negative things an opponent has done. Even if there were not campaign budget limits, voters are not interested in absorbing large amounts of information about each candidate. The combination of limited budgets and limited electoral interest means that campaigns must decide what to emphasize. The goal of a campaign is to win the election. Obtaining reactions from voters about the impact of specific information about a candidate and an opponent helps a campaign decide what to focus on. If voters are most impressed by the military record of a candidate and most distressed about a particular vote or issue position of an opponent, the campaign should focus on those matters. Polling helps sort out what to focus on.

To sort out the role of potential issues, campaigns begin by initially discussing all the traits, votes, and positions that might sway voters and help win the election or cause them to lose it. They then discuss how visible is each issue, do the two candidates differ in a clear way, have the media covered the issue, can they think of an effective and simple way to create a contrast. Decisions have to be made that some issues are more important than others and should be asked about in a poll.

This probing for the significance of issues or the traits of candidates can be done in two ways. A poll can ask about the significance of candidate traits, without attaching specific candidate names to the traits. Or, the campaign can present specific positions or actions of a candidate and ask if knowing that makes them more or less likely to vote for the candidate.

The first approach is most valuable when a candidate is relatively unknown and the concern is, in presenting the candidate to voters, what aspects of her background will be seen most positively and which will be seen most negatively. The emphasis in the presentation will then be on those aspects seen positively, and responses to those seen negatively will be developed in case the opponent decides to focus on them. Table 4.9 presents an example of the kind of general traits that might be asked about, without mentioning the candidate's name. These traits should not just be any general traits, but ones that the candidate possesses.

Table 4.9   Assessing Candidate Traits

Q. Now I'd like to try something different. I'll read you traits a candidate for public office might have, and for each trait please tell me if you would be more or less likely to vote for someone with that trait. If it won't make any difference, please say so.

Would you be more or less likely to vote for a candidate who . . .

	More Likely	No Difference	Less Likely	No Opinion
Q. Is a lawyer	1	2	3	4
Q. Is a former teacher and school principal	1	2	3	4
Q. Is in his thirties	1	2	3	4
Q. Is in his seventies	1	2	3	4
Q. Is opposed to gun control laws	1	2	3	4
Q. Is in favor of tougher standards for schools	1	2	3	4
Q. Thinks the solution to school problems is more money	1	2	3	4
Q. Has been elected to several local offices	1	2	3	4
Q. Has never held an elective position	1	2	3	4
Q. Is endorsed by the governor	1	2	3	4
Q. Is pro-choice on the abortion issue	1	2	3	4

The second approach is to connect specific positions to candidates to determine what positions, actions, or aspects of the background of the candidate will be helpful and which might cause problems. This second approach is more common when a candidate has been in office and is relatively well known. Campaigns regularly test for candidate vulnerability by presenting negative information about their own candidate to determine if opponent attacks about the issue are likely to have an effect. If the polling shows that the electorate is bothered by something, it is crucial to develop a response to the criticism. If the electorate shows no sign of being troubled by a criticism, then the campaign can ignore attacks by an opponent. They also, of course, follow the same practice in assessing the vulnerabilities of the opponent.

Table 4.10 presents examples of questions a campaign might ask. Assume that the poll is being done for candidate A, who is being challenged in a primary by candidate B. Voters are presented with both negative and positive information about each candidate. With regard to A, positive and negative information is presented. In the positive area, the candidate has won the party designation and needs to know if voters see this positively. If so, this can be stressed in all literature. If it doesn't matter, or even creates a negative impression, it is best to not waste any resources presenting this. In an effort to anticipate a problem, candidate A brings up his age of seventy to see if it matters to voters. If so, then it is essential to avoid pictures or images that indicate his age. The pro-life position of A is also included to see if this presents problems.

Table 4.10 Assessing Candidate Strengths and Weaknesses

Q. Next I'd like to tell you just a few specifics about each candidate and ask if each makes you more likely to support (candidate A) or (candidate B), or if it makes no difference.

	Support A	No Difference	Support B	No Opinion
Q. Democratic Party committee members met recently and designated A as their party nominee over B.	1	2	3	4
Q. B is a successful businessman, while A has been in office for sixteen years and has never worked in the private sector.	1	2	3	4
Q. A has been elected to several local offices—town council and county legislature—while B has never run for office.	1	2	3	4
Q. A is 70 and B is 38.	1	2	3	4
Q. A is a life-long Democrat, while B recently changed his party registration from Republican to Democrat.	1	2	3	4
Q. A is pro-choice while B is pro-life.	1	2	3	4

Voters are also given information about B that might be used by A against him. B has no experience in office, and it is important to know if voters care about that. B also recently changed his party registration and it might be possible to criticize him as an opportunist. The poll results will indicate whether this recent change matters to people.

The results will also indicate if the information troubles very specific voters (older, do not vote regularly, etc.) and if a targeted message can be sent to these voters. The question about age, for example, might indicate that older voters are not troubled, and, indeed, are much more likely to vote for A when presented with the age difference. Younger voters, in contrast, might be more inclined to vote for the younger candidate. Since age is a trait of voters that is known, older voters can be selected from the registration rolls and a specific mailing can be sent to them that conveys the differences in the age and experience of the two candidates. Younger registrants are unlikely to hear about this age emphasis, unless the piece ends up in the press, and even if they do it is unlikely to have a negative effect because younger registrants vote at lower rates.

Candidates use such push questions during campaigns, but also when specific events occur that might create problems for an incumbent. The incumbent might have accepted a gift or a trip that could look bad. A relative may have gotten a special government benefit. An elected official may then ask for a poll, after a brief period of time to allow press coverage of the event to evolve, to see if the event has registered. The questions below (table 4.11) are to assess if voters have followed the issue, who they hold responsible, and if it affects the mayor's standing among voters. If it does, then it indicates the mayor has to address the issue or it will cause him problems.

Table 4.11   Assessing Potential Problems

Q. During the last week, did you hear, read, or see anything about a government benefit involving [name]?

   1 ___ yes   2 ___ no   3 ___ not sure / no response

Q. (Only if yes) Do you see this as something the mayor should be responsible for, or as the responsibility of the city official in charge of this program? (Record both if offered.)

   1 ___ mayor   2 ___ city official   3 ___ both   4 ___ no opinion

Q. Does the incident make you more or less favorable toward the Mayor? (record no difference)

   1 ___ more   2 ___ no difference   3 ___ less   4 ___ no opinion

In summary, push polling, in the sense of planting inaccurate and damaging information, is rarely done. Push polling, in the sense of presenting positive and negative facts and seeing which ones "push" people to vote differently, is a regular practice. It is used to assess positive and negative information for both the candidate and the opponent. The information helps campaigns decide what issues to focus on. It is not a means to manipulate the electorate. Indeed, it involves asking voters what matters to them and then using that feedback to create messages to affect the campaign outcome.

Demographics

After issues have been asked about, questions about demographics are included. The questions that should be included depend on the source of the data on potential respondents. If the initial source is the registration files of the local Board of Elections (however named), these files will generally contain the individual's party identification or registration, place of residence, sex, and age. The files often contain the voting record (how frequently a person votes). If these are present, then it is not necessary to include these at the end of the survey. If not, it is essential to ask questions about these matters.

Aside from these questions, there is often a debate about what other matters should be asked about. Sometimes there is a healthy tension between the campaign manager and the pollster about asking about identifiable and nonidentifiable traits of voters. The goal of a poll is to identify those who support a candidate and those who do not. Ideally, the identification should be done in such a way that those who create electronic ads and distribute direct mail (usually different people) can then use that information to find the identified voters and get a message to them. For example, campaign managers may wish to know if a male Republican candidate is having trouble winning the support of women. Knowing this, the campaign can place ads on radio stations or television shows that attract this audience to try to get a message to them. Or a direct mail letter can be sent to women. If Independent women in particular are not supportive, then all women who are likely voters can be pulled from a voter registration file, and a letter from a prominent woman supporter can be sent to them.

While campaign managers and consultants may wish to have data that connect voter support (or lack thereof) to an identifiable trait, the traits of sex, age, or party registration are unlikely to capture all the sources of divisions that are crucial to the campaign. There is considerable evidence that there are other important factors that create electoral divisions, and these factors are not readily identifiable. Liberals and conservatives are increasingly divided in their support for the parties (Abramowitz 1994; Abramowitz and Saunders 1998, 2000). Racial divisions have been important since the 1960s (Carmines and

Stimson 1989). Class divisions have grown in recent years (Stonecash 2000; Stonecash, Brewer, et al. 2000; Brewer and Stonecash 2001). Union membership generally inclines people to be more supportive of Democrats. Religion still matters, with Catholics more inclined to vote Democratic than Protestants (Brewer 2003), and traditionalists more conservative than secularists (Layman 2001). Working women and families with children in school are often different in their partisan support than others.

While all these are potential sources of political division, it is never possible to know which will be important in a specific campaign before conducting a poll. To know which divisions are important, it is necessary to ask questions about the respondent's political philosophy, religion, union membership, and many other issues. That prompts a pollster and campaign manager to want to include more questions. This solution is not always welcome, however, for two very important reasons. First, the campaign manager and other consultants may argue that it is not possible to identify liberals or conservatives in the electorate, or union members, or the less affluent, in order to convey to them a message. This inability to specifically identify voters by some known trait will make it impossible to rely on targeted mailings or to run ads on specific radio stations. For these reasons, some campaign managers will be reluctant to include questions about these traits.

While not being able to identify specific people is a problem, this does not mean that questions about political philosophy, union membership, children in school, or work status should not be asked. The crosstabs may be very valuable in alerting the campaign that the candidate is losing voters with particular views. Self-identified moderates may be voting fairly strongly for the opponent. Those who are pro-choice may not be as strong as the candidate hopes. Working women may show weak support for a male Republican candidate. It is important to try to win more of those voters; if they are sizeable within the district, it is then possible to run general ads or send a blanket mailing to get the message across that the candidate is not opposed to a particular concern.

While it is possible to ask numerous questions about possible sources of political divisions, the second reason campaigns often are reluctant to including an extensive number of questions about demographics and various opinions is financial. More questions create longer surveys, which cost more money, and the campaign may not be able to afford the cost. If all these demographic questions are asked, it may be necessary to drop questions about very specific issues that may be relevant for the campaign. As with all these issues, it is important to discuss with the candidate and the campaign manager what sources of political divisions might be relevant so the decision of what to include and exclude is a mutual one. These decisions are never final, of course. It might be possible to include many questions in the initial benchmark and continue only with questions about those traits that appear to be of some relevance. If a campaign cannot afford many questions at the beginning but is able to raise more money as the campaign progresses, it may be possible to increase the number of questions later in the campaign to thoroughly assess the factors affecting vote choice.

Once the decision is made to ask about demographics and respondent opinions, the questions should be asked so that the least intrusive and personal questions are asked first, with the most intrusive ones asked last. For example, asking about marital status, whether someone has been unemployed, economic situation in recent years, and family income is intrusive to some people and should be the last questions asked. This will minimize the risk of alienating respondents earlier in the survey, and if they object, it will come right at the end of the survey and not result in the loss of any information.

Open-Ended versus Closed-Ended Questions

The use of closed-ended questions troubles many for two reasons. First, their use means that respondents are presented with options chosen by others. If respondents do not like the options, which they sometimes do not, there is no means for an alternative response to be expressed or recorded. The result is that an opinion is not captured, and the caller may respond by placing the response in the "no opinion" category, which misrepresents the person. Second, the campaign may not wish to suggest any responses but allow people to use their own language and mention the issues important to them without any guidance.

The first problem, imposed and restricted choices, is one to take seriously. As noted above, if responses do not match with the concerns of voters, the results will not tell the campaign what voters are really thinking. The best way to avoid this problem is to follow the process discussed earlier. The pollster should work closely with political people to make sure the alternative responses do a good job capturing the primary alternatives that exist on an issue. If this is done carefully, there will be very few people who object to the choices presented.

The virtue of the approach of providing alternative answers is that these responses are *much* easier to work with in conducting an analysis of the opinions driving vote choices. It is possible to do crosstabs[8] with closed-ended responses, while it is time consuming and very difficult to code open-ended responses to reduce them to responses that can be used for crosstabs.

While open-ended questions can have their limits, there are specific situations in which they are very valuable. Campaigns use them when they want to see how voters react without any guidance from a caller or a script (Geer 1991). Campaigns often use this approach for asking about local problems, how a candidate is seen, or what information voters recall about a campaign. Table 4.12 provides examples.

The first question asks what voters think is the most important problem. It is an example of a precoded open-ended question. The precoding makes it easier for callers to classify and record responses. The second question is intended to get an idea of the association voters have with a candidate. This helps early on to provide information on whether voters have much of an image of a candidate and what that image is. The third question is to determine if an incumbent has problems. The last question is to find out what messages voters are picking up as the campaign proceeds. It helps the campaign know if the intended message is getting across or voters are picking up something else.

Even in these situations, however, the results are often disappointing to the campaign. Voters are often inarticulate in this situation. They have not had time to think about the question, and they may wish to get the survey over as fast as possible. They may blurt something out that a caller tries to capture, but the statement may not be very coherent. While that is a problem with some questions, in other cases the inability to articulate something provides valuable information. For questions about the image of the candidate or hesitations about reelecting an incumbent, the most important matter may be how many or how few voters offer a response. Even if inarticulate, if a large proportion of likely voters offers some reason why they are hesi-

Table 4.12   Open-Ended Questions

Q. What do you think is the most important issue facing your community at this time? *(Do not read the list; record only one response; if more than one offered, ask "which is most important?")*

1 ___ jobs/lack of jobs/
     economy
2 ___ taxes/property taxes/
     income taxes
3 ___ education
4 ___ environment
5 ___ crime/drugs

6 ___ health care
7 ___ welfare
8 ___ declining moral values
9 ___ youth leaving the area
     for jobs
10 ___ housing costs
11 ___ Other *(record)* _____

Q. When you think of (candidate), what comes to mind?

Q. If you have one hesitation about reelecting (candidate), what would it be?

Q. What do you recall hearing, seeing, or reading about the campaign within the last two weeks?

---

tant about reelecting someone, it indicates that the candidate has problems. If few have any hesitations, it is a sign the electorate cannot recall any negative thoughts about the incumbent.

Information and the ``Informed'' Ballot

In formulating a campaign plan, a major problem is trying to anticipate the impact of presenting information to voters. Campaign managers would like to know how specific information will be received and how much it will affect voters' choices. Will the candidate's specific legislative votes or positions taken on issues affect how people vote? Will it matter to voters that one candidate is pro-choice and the other is pro-life? Will it matter that one candidate has never run for office before and that the other has won numerous offices? Will it matter that the experienced candidate is much older than the other? Will endorsements matter? One way to try to assess the role of information is to engage in an "informed ballot" test. After the matchup has been asked about, respondents can then be presented with a summary of the primary traits and positions of the candidates. Then the matchup can be asked again. Those respondents who change can also be asked directly what information made them change.

If this exercise is to be of any value, it is necessary to balance the information presented. If the information is slanted, respondents will become suspicious and even object to the exercise. Most importantly, if the information is not balanced and reflective of the kinds of information that will come out during the campaign from both candidates, the information derived will be of no value to the campaign. Slanted information will produce biased results and create false hopes of what can happen during a campaign.

An example of such an exercise, using balanced information, is presented in table 4.13. The poll is being done for Smith. Several positive comments are made about him, followed by positive comments about Jones. In the course of mentioning Jones, his age of seventy-two is given. This provides information that may be relevant to some voters (making some positive to Jones and others negative). Then Jones's criticisms of Smith are presented. The intent is to see if voters will respond to criticisms of Smith, who is from a wealthy, well-connected family. This information is followed by a repeat of the matchup and, if they change their choice, a follow-up question about why they changed.

If respondents change their choice, it is then possible to determine what category of voters move from one choice to another. If, for example, Independents change a great deal from the initial to the informed ballot, it suggests anticipating this criticism and its impact during the campaign and have a plan to avoid this impact.

While these exercises are very valuable, they can also be delusional. Candidates sometimes read a situation of significant change and assume they will be able to get their message out and achieve the results shown in the exercise. Some candidates do not understand that the results will occur only if they raise money and get their message out. Others simply do not like to ask for money, and they never acquire the resources to have an impact.

Table 4.13   Creating an Informed Ballot

Q. Now I'd like to tell you a few things that are likely to come up during the Assembly campaign. Harry Smith will stress that he lives in County A and works in County B, so he knows both communities in the Assembly district very well. He will point out that he is a Republican with close ties to the governor and that will help him get things done.

Joe Jones will stress that, despite being seventy-two years old, he will be effective because, as a Democrat, he will be in the majority, and he will be able to bring state money to his district, much like the former Assembly member Robinson used to do. He will say that Harry Smith is just a member of a wealthy family who is using his family's money and political connections to gain public office, and Smith has no political experience.

Now that you've had a chance to learn a little about the campaign, could I ask again, with the candidates Harry Smith, the Republican, and Joe Jones, the Democrat, will you most likely vote for Smith or Jones?

   1 __ Smith   2 __ Jones   3 __ Undecided

Q. *(If changed from prior matchup Q)*: I notice that you changed your choice. Could you tell me what caused you to change?
   1 __ Smith is from County A
   2 __ Smith knows both communities
   3 __ Smith has ties to (the governor)
   4 __ Smith is connected to a wealthy family
   5 __ Smith has no political experience
   6 __ Jones is seventy-two
   7 __ Jones will be in the majority
   8 __ Jones is endorsed by Robinson
   9 __ No opinion given

Creating a Coherent Sequence to the Questions

As noted earlier, surveys generally have a standard sequence of name identification, matchups, issues, and then demographics. It is also important to make sure that all of the issue questions that are decided upon have an overall coherence to them. It helps respondents if questions are organized as follows. Questions about the same topic should be bunched together so the respondent can focus on that topic before moving to another one. Questions about a specific topic should proceed from general to more specific questions. For example, if there is concern about schools and the issue questions focus on funding and standards, it is helpful to start with a general question about rating or assessing the performance of schools, followed by a question about the adequacy of funding, support for higher standards, and then maybe one about which of the last two is likely to be most important to affecting school performance.

The Pretesting Issue

Campaign polling is different from many academic polls. In academic polls, the initial script is pretested by calling a small number of respondents. Very often, the respondents are then interviewed to ask them their interpretation of the questions. They are also asked to offer general comments on the questions and suggest revisions. After this, those conducting the survey may subject the responses to statistical tests to determine if responses are consistent and associated with other responses as expected. The survey is then revised and then implemented. These steps are to make sure that the pollster and the respondent agree on what the question is asking. If there is agreement, then there is much greater confidence in the results.

Campaign polling rarely involves these steps. The campaign does not wish to let the other side know they are doing polling. Pollsters do not wish to have to divulge to respondents who is doing the poll, so they do not wish to go through a process of indicating who is doing a poll and asking respondents to critique the script. Perhaps most important, the academic approach is time consuming and expensive, and campaigns do not wish to spend the money or the time. Campaigns want secrecy and quick turnaround. For all these reasons, pollsters rely on their knowledge of how to ask questions, discussions with campaign managers, and their instincts about how to ask questions. The academic steps are admirable and to be respected, but campaigns cannot afford the luxury.

Notes

1. "Push polling" is also a term used to call voters and, under the guise of polling, plant negative information about opponents. That will be discussed later.

"Push" is used here in the sense of getting respondents to make or reveal a choice.

2. I was once involved in a mayoral campaign in which the mayoral candidate included a matchup question about the president of the City Council. The results indicated that the incumbent president was losing, in a city in which Democrats had a significant enrollment advantage. After I presented the results to the candidates, I was leaving the headquarters when the president of the Council stopped me in front of others and began to loudly and publicly berate me about how inaccurate my results were and how I did not know what I was doing. I explained the process again and left it at that. He persisted in making a very public issue out of it, and I eventually excused myself and left. The incumbent eventually lost. During the year after that, a number of people stopped me and told me that they were impressed about my accuracy and my willingness to calmly stick with the unpleasant results without getting into an argument. Delivering bad but accurate news does not hurt a reputation. Most politicians can live with negative information, but they want to be able to trust you about the accuracy of results.

3. In New York, Indian tribes have won lawsuits versus governments about the illegal selling of their lands. While the decisions are often unpopular, most politicians appear to have accepted the decisions of the courts and do not want to inflame public opinion about the issue. Several have said to just drop questions about the issue because it is settled.

4. I have found that candidates generally veto questions about personal problems of their opponent because they say they will not use it, so why gather it. One opponent had been charged with sexual misconduct, and the story had appeared in the newspapers several years prior, but the candidate said he wouldn't attack his opponent about the issue, so no questions were to be asked. In another case, the prior spouse of an opponent had filed charges of adultery in a divorce proceeding. The race was expected to be close, but the candidate vetoed questions about the issue because he did not want to use that kind of criticism during the campaign. In other cases, information may not involve personal matters but involve a policy option that the candidate does not feel is responsible. In a situation involving Indian land claims, the candidate did not want to even ask about resisting a court order. He did not want to encourage such a view and would not advocate such an option, no matter how popular.

5. There is some research showing that when respondents are presented with two competing views and asked which they agree with, this brings out divisions more. When questions are put as assertive statements and voters are asked if they agree or disagree with the assertion, they are less likely to divide as much (Bolstein 1991). Despite that, assertive statements are a regular part of campaign polls to test whether statements a candidate might make will be met with agreement or disagreement.

6. This occurred in a campaign I was working. The polling firm of the opponent presented information that my candidate had been cited by state agencies for failing to follow required business practices some years before. A respondent

then called a newspaper. After a reporter pursued the claim, it was discovered that the initial state agency complaint against the candidate had been a result of a record mistake on the part of the state agency. The result was several days of stories about this campaign tactic and about how the instigating campaign had not done its research properly. The instigating campaign had to apologize for using the question and the tactic, and it was further embarrassed about not getting its facts straight. There was no benefit for the campaign and lots of bad press coverage.

7. The bibliography contains a set of stories about this controversy, under the title *Push Polling in the 2000 Election*.

8. Crosstabs, to be explained in detail later, present data in a way that indicates how those with differing views vote or how their views on another issue are distributed.

Pulling a Sample: Who Votes, Sample Size, and Representativeness

W HEN CONDUCTING A POLL, two decisions must be made about sampling. The first decision involves whose opinions the candidate wants to know, which means who should be screened out of the process. The second decision involves anticipating the volume of refusals, bad numbers, and people not at home at the time calling is conducted and trying to gauge how big the initial call list should be. The former involves the serious issue of who counts politically, while the second involves the more mundane but important matter of managing the calling process.

Voting and Who to Include in the Process

Campaigns want to contact and assess the opinions and vote choices of those likely to vote in a particular election. When a sample of people to call is drawn, it is essential to begin with a list of only those likely to vote in that election. There is a regular pattern as to who follows politics and votes. Interest in campaigns and voting frequency increase correspondingly with such traits as age and education (Couper 1997; Flanigan and Zingale 2002; Day and Gaither 2000; Jamieson, et al. 2002). Turnout also varies with the timing of elections.

Age is a particularly important trait, because it significantly affects turnout and it is usually recorded in voter registration files. This makes it possible, if voting records are also kept in the files, to analyze voting patterns in an area to make judgments about future voting patterns. Age and the timing of an election (whether presidential or midterm) combine to affect who should be called in any particular election year. The patterns shown in table 5.1 present an example of differences in turnout by age and by type of election from the registration files of a

County Board of Elections. The figures are the percentages of those within an age group, among those registered to vote, who actually voted.[1] Boards use the information on voting frequency to decide whether to leave someone in the file from year to year. States are not required to keep people on the rolls forever, and a continual record of nonvoting can be used to eliminate someone.

Table 5.1   Age and Voting: General and by Type of Election (Results from a County Registration File)

Age	Distribution of Voting Frequency Over Last Six General Elections (sum across to 100 for each row)				Percent Voting for Specific Election Years		
	0	1–3	4–5	6	1998	2000	2001
18–29	44.6	50.1	4.5	0.8	11.6	44.9	11.2
30–44	23.4	47.1	19.3	10.2	39.9	69.1	27.3
45–59	10.6	35.9	29.6	23.9	63.9	84.4	42.8
60 plus	5.9	21.0	31.0	42.1	78.9	88.2	60.0

The columns in the left side of the table record the percentage of those in an age group who voted in 0, 1–3, 4–5, and 6 of the last 6 general elections. Among those aged 18–29, 44.6 percent have no record of voting over the last 6 years. Some of this is to be expected because these individuals may have just registered. Among those 60 and over, only 5.9 percent have no record of voting, and 53.1 percent voted in every election. The significance of this is that those who are younger are less likely to vote. They are more mobile and less integrated into the life of the adult community. They follow the news less—they are less likely to read a daily newspaper or to watch a television news program (Witt 2002, 29). As they age they may follow the pattern of other older registrants and vote more, but there is evidence that younger people now follow politics less than young people did thirty years ago (Witt 2002, 30). Regardless, for any current campaign the important matter is that younger registrants are less likely to vote.

This pattern is not fixed, however. It varies by the type of election. Presidential elections receive much more attention in the media and are widely presented as having much more significance in our society. The heightened coverage increases the interest of all voters, and particularly of those who are younger. The consequence is that in a presidential election year younger people turn out at much higher levels.

The right side of the table indicates the percentage with a history of voting in a specific year. For a presidential year (2000), the difference in voting rates for those aged 18–29 and those over 60 is 43 percentage points. In nonpresidential years, and in odd-numbered years (usually called "off-off" years), the differences increase to 67 and 49 percentage points, respectively.

The consequence of these patterns is that campaigns know that not everyone is equally inclined to vote, even in a presidential year. The electorate that votes and that a candidate has to worry about will be different in a presidential year from the pool of those registered. In an off-year the actual electorate will be even more different from all registrants.

The following example (table 5.2) indicates how much the composition changes. The column on the left indicates the actual composition of all registrants, by age group, for a county Board of Elections registration file. The next two columns indicate recorded turnout rates by age groups for the presidential year, and the percentage of all voters coming from each age group (composition). Those under 30 are 14.8 percent of all registrants in the file, but they are only 8.9 percent of those who have a history of voting in 2000. For the 1998 election, only 3.2 percent have a record of voting. Older voters—over 60—are more likely to have a history of voting. In this case, while those over 60 are 27 percent of all registrants, they are 40 percent of those with a history of voting in 1998. In an off-year, the differentials in turnout are greater, and the composition of those with a record of voting is much different from the file of all registrants.

These differences have enormous consequences for polling and for politics in general. With regard to the latter, the existence of this information, which is increasingly available in readily accessible computer

Table 5.2   Turnout and the Composition of the Electorate

Age	All Actual Registrants	Presidential (2000)		Off-Year (1998)	
		Turnout	Composition	Turnout	Composition
18–29	14.8	44.9	8.9	11.6	3.2
30–44	29.2	69.1	26.8	39.9	21.9
45–59	29.1	84.4	32.6	63.9	34.9
60 plus	27.0	88.2	31.7	78.9	40.0

format, means that candidates can discern who is likely to vote and focus on those likely voters. These files can be used to select only those with records of voting regularly, then sorted by street and house number, so that door-to-door walks can focus only on those likely to vote. It also means that direct mail can be sent only to those likely to vote.

When conducting a poll, the desire is to eliminate those who are unlikely to vote. Either before calling is begun, or during the calling process, those unlikely to vote should be screened. There are two ways to screen voters to make sure the initial list of people to call reflects those likely to vote in a particular year. The best way is to use voter registration lists that record how frequently people vote. If voting over the last several years is recorded, then the complete file can be acquired, and a sample can be drawn of all those voting a certain number of times over the last several elections. If it is a presidential election year, then those voting less frequently can be included.

If it is a local election, in an off-off year, then only regular voters should be selected. The rules for selecting registrants should be clearly stated to the campaign manager and the candidate so they know who is being contacted and who is being eliminated. If a voter registration file exists, with voting records, it is best to analyze the entire file and summarize differences in voting rates by age and present these to the campaign manager. Then it is important to review the turnout rates in similarly scheduled elections in the past and assess whether the current election is likely to attract much attention. If this is a low-visibility election, with no high-visibility state-level election, then turnout is likely to be less and fewer registrants should be included. If the race could attract a lot of attention, or there is a close gubernatorial or U.S. Senate race, more registrants should be included.

Decisions also have to be made about recent registrants and recent voting records. Someone may have a record of little voting, but if the file shows that she just registered in the current year, this may be a reflection of interest and she should therefore be included. This is particularly important during a presidential year, when registration increases a great deal. It is also valuable to assess the total number of recorded votes and recency of voting over the last two to three years. Registration rules usually allow someone to miss several years before being purged from the rolls. If someone has voted three out of the last six years, but has not voted over the last three years, with one of those a presidential year, he may have moved and should not be included in the sample selected.

After all these matters have been discussed, the pollster and the campaign manager can settle on a rule for selecting registrants for a sample.[2] Assuming turnout might be relatively high, the rule might be to include all those voting in two or more of the last six general elections, plus all those all registering in the current year, minus all those not voting in the last three years. If the election is likely to attract a lower turnout, the rule might be changed to all those voting in three of the last six years, plus the other criteria. Settling on this rule should be carefully discussed, because it is important, unless conditions change, to stay with this rule, so that sample results are comparable from one poll to another. No candidate wants to be presented with the statement that "the difference could be because we called a different sample of registrants."

Sometimes registration files and voter history are not available. Such files may not be in a format that is easily accessible or may not include voter history. If voter registration files are not available, an alternative source is national firms that will sell lists with names and telephone numbers to the campaign. Firms continually process voter registration lists for states that have registration. They also continually buy and assess telephone book lists of numbers to see if they are representative of the population in an area.[3] If a campaign must rely on these less than ideal files, then it is necessary to screen possible respondents to ask their level of interest in the campaign and their likelihood of voting. Those with little interest or inclination to vote are dropped before an interview begins.

If a firm provides telephone numbers with the name used for the listing, the process becomes more complicated. Husbands are listed more often than wives, so the caller cannot just ask for the name listed, or males will be overrepresented. In these cases, or cases in which just a number is available, it is necessary to use some method to randomly access people in the household. A common method is to ask for the adult over eighteen who will have the next birthday, or the one who had the most recent birthday. Then it is necessary to do extensive screening about whether the person is registered and how interested she is in the election. If it is necessary to screen, table 5.3 is an example of the kinds of questions asked. A person who passes the three hurdles of being registered, voting frequently, and being interested in this campaign is likely to vote in this election.

Table 5.3   Screening Questions

Q. Are you currently registered to vote in this (county / city)?
  1 ___ Yes (continue)
  2 ___ No (*then indicate*): Thanks, that's all. We appreciate your time.

Q. Would you say you usually vote, roughly half the time, or vote only occasionally?
  1 ___ Usually (continue)
  2 ___ Half (continue)
  3 ___ Occasionally (*then indicate*): Thanks, that's all. We appreciate your time.

Q. How interested are you in the current campaign: very, somewhat, not much?
  1 ___ Very (continue)
  2 ___ Somewhat (continue)
  3 ___ Not much (*then indicate*): Thanks, that's all. We appreciate your time.

While these questions help screen out those who are definitely not registered and definitely not interested, there is always concern whether this approach screens strictly enough. Someone who has not voted very often may still think he is registered when he is not. Many people are reluctant to indicate that they have no interest in an upcoming election, so there it is likely that some people will say they are interested when they are not really that interested. I have used questions about interest and compared them with actual voting frequency from voter registration files. The results indicate that those who say they are less interested do vote less frequently, but the cross-tabs also indicate that many people who say they are interested are less frequent voters. Screening voters when starting with just telephone numbers is not easy, and it is a regular matter of discussions regarding national polls (Crespi 1988; Erikson 1993; Voss, et al. 1995; Freedman and Goldstein 1996).

Sample Size

Once a decision is made about whom to contact, the next decision is how many people to actually interview, which affects how big the initial list of potential respondents should be. Sample size is one of the most visible, but perhaps most overrated, aspects of polling. Most candidates and campaign managers worry that a smaller sample size will produce unreliable results, so there is anxiety about whether a sample should be larger. In reality, sample size is only one of many factors that affect the validity of polls. For a poll to be valid, the right questions must be asked and asked in appropriate ways. The issue of whom to sample must be carefully considered. Then there is the issue of sample size. If the first steps—questions and sampling—are not done properly, the results may be biased, and the size of the sample of contacted respondents will not make the results valid.

The rules for deciding on sample size are relatively simple. Any sampling process is likely to have some error. Speaking with a relatively small segment of the public, even if done randomly, can result in a slight over- or underrepresentation of some views in the community. The larger the size of the sample, the less is the probability that some segment of the population is over- or underrepresented. When a small sample is contacted (for example, 100 people), random chance could result in some group with specific views being too large a portion of the sample, relative to their presence in the population. Too many men might be contacted, and men may be more favorable to the candidate. As the sample size increases, the process of contacting a random sample results in men being an appropriate percentage in the contacted sample, and the sample becomes more representative of the population. When a sample gets to about 300, statistical theory tells us that a sample of that size will produce results with a likely margin of error of about 6 percentage points. That is, the actual results within the population could be within a range of 6 points lower or 6 points higher of the results found in the poll. If a candidate gets 50 percent of the vote in the sample, her actual percentage in the electorate could be from 45 percent to 55 percent. As the sample size increases to 400, the margin of error, or possible divergence of the reported from the actual, declines to plus or minus 5 percentage points. For a sample of 500, the margin of error declines to about 4 percentage points.[4]

The obvious desire of any campaign is to have the greatest confidence in results, which leads to the desire to have larger samples. The limit, of course, is cost versus the small gain in confidence that occurs with a greater sample size. A sample of 400 costs more than a sample of 300. To reduce the margin of error to plus or minus 3, the sample size must go to over 600, which costs much more. For most campaigns, since pollsters generally charge for a combination of the number of questions and the sample size, the only way to achieve a larger sample size is to reduce the number of questions. That deprives the campaign of information just to achieve a 1 to 2 percentage point gain in confidence in the actual numbers.

The essential issue here is the purpose of a poll. The goal is not to predict an outcome of an election. While there is considerable attention on the "horse race" in national presidential polls and how well they predict the outcome, the goal of campaign polling is to find out who supports the candidate and who does not. This provides information to the campaign about what messages to get to whom. It is far more important for campaigns to ask more questions and live with a reasonable margin of error. For most campaigns, a sample of 300, with a margin of error of 5 percentage points, is quite adequate. If all the prior steps have been done correctly, information about which voters need to be reinforced and which need to get a message is more important. *Indeed, if the campaign does its job and gets the right message to voters who are moveable and they change their choice, the final results will be different from those shown in a poll, and the poll will have achieved its purpose.*

While 300 is a normal sample size, there are situations in which a larger sample may be desired. The margin of error figures indicated above also applies to specific sample groups. If a candidate is running in a jurisdiction that includes distinctly different communities, then the desire may be to have a sample for each community that has a reasonable margin of error. For example, if two candidates are running for a state legislative district that encompasses two counties, each county home to one of the candidates, it may be desirable to have a sample in each county that is of sufficient size to indicate with reasonable confidence what the results are. To acquire a sample of 300 within each county is expensive, so the campaign may decide on 200 per county for a total of 400. Each situation is unique and needs to be discussed.

Again, while it is desirable to have large samples, the process of writing questions and drawing samples is probably more important than sample sizes. The difficulty in telling candidates that they can live with a smaller sample is that sample size has an association with statistical validity, which prompts most nonstatisticians to be anxious about being scientific. The attention of the campaign should focus on the first phases of the polling process and the analysis of the results.

Once the desired sample size is determined, it is then possible to work backwards to determine the size of the initial list of potential respondents. Any calling process will result in a large volume of incompletes. There will be refusals, numbers that no longer connect with the listed person because they have moved or died, and many people who are not home at the time of the call.[5] In addition to these traditional sources of noncompletion, technology is creating more factors that can intervene and affect the ability to contact possible respondents and create a representative sample. Many people use Caller I.D. or answering machines to screen calls, and many are unwilling to take a call from a source they do not recognize. The callers may reach homes where the person is home, but the person uses either of these devices to screen the call and does not answer.[6] Younger people are more likely to use these methods to screen, creating the possibility that it will lower their participation rate and result in their underrepresention (Link and Oldendick 1999). Among younger people there is the new phenomenon of their exclusive use of a cell phone as their telephone account. I know of no studies of whether this increases or decreases the ability to contact possible respondents and affects their willingness to participate. There is apparently also an increase in the percentage of families who have second phones for computer lines or for children. Whether this affects the ability to contact potential respondents is also unknown.

All these factors have the potential to reduce the ability to contact individuals despite having a telephone number. To make sure that the list is not exhausted before the desired number of interviews (sample size) is reached, it is necessary to pull an initial list of potential respondents much larger than the desired sample and then cycle through it in a random fashion. Refusal rates and the extent of mobility are not the same across the county, so the initial size will vary by area, and anyone working in a region needs to have some sense of how local conditions vary.[7]

If the list is taken from registration files, the enactment of the

Motor Voter bill by Congress has affected the size of the initial call list that must be created. The Motor Voter bill was enacted in an effort to get more people to register and vote. The bill provided that registration forms had to be made widely available at government agency offices. While I have not seen specific studies of who takes advantage of this bill, over time this provision has resulted in a great number of people being added to the rolls. Many of these registrants appear to be less interested and more likely to move over time. The process of screening for regularity of voting removes many of them from the initial sample, but many are still included in samples. Those who move more will fall into the category of "no longer at that number," which means there will not be a completion. Because there are many in this group, it is necessary to increase the initial sample size to anticipate the noncompletions.

With all these factors considered, a decision must be made about the size of the initial sample. It is better to have too big a sample so that the calling process (to be discussed in the next chapter) does not culminate in repeated attempts to call those not contacted. To achieve a contacted sample of 300, I generally pull an initial call list (sample) of 2,500 to 3,000. For 400, I pull somewhere between 3,500 and 4,000 registrants. If the calling is done using a sample of telephone numbers, the initial sample must be still larger because many people will not be registered and will not be interested in the campaign.

Finally, it is crucial to avoid introducing any disruption of the randomness of a sample when giving the list to callers. The best way to avoid bias is to make sure the lists of those to be called are not sorted by geography or likelihood of voting. If this sorting occurred and some callers were much better at achieving completions than others (which always happens), the people from one area or with a greater tendency to vote might become a relatively greater portion of the final sample and perhaps bias the results. To make sure the names are randomly listed, sort alphabetically by last names. This scrambles the names so there is no particular order. With this randomness, it will not matter if one caller is more successful than another while calling.

Assessing Representativeness

Once the calling process is done and the report is being prepared, it is important to be able to tell the candidate and the campaign how representative the sample is of the population of voters the campaign wants to focus on. That is, of likely voters a certain percentage is Republican, Independent, or Democrat. Once the sample of completed interviews is acquired, the question is whether the sample of 300 has a distribution of party registration for respondents similar to the profile of all likely voters. It is crucial before reviewing results with a campaign to address the issue of the representativeness of the sample. Many times candidates are skeptical of the results. If there are doubts about the wording of the questions, that concern may be legitimate. Many times, however, the skepticism stems from a belief that the sample must be biased, or that it includes relatively too many Democrats or Republicans. This can then lead to a suggestion that the poll is not to be trusted because of the bias issue. The best way to end that line of argument before it begins is to review the sample and compare it to the initial sample pulled before reviewing the poll results. Candidates generally do not like to spend time reviewing this aspect, but it is important to do that. There will always be some discrepancies, but differences of 2 to 4 percentage points are normal and should not be a cause for doubting the validity of the results.

Below is a typical summary sheet I prepare and include as a part of every poll report. It tells the campaign how the sample was selected (who was included and who was eliminated) and when the poll was conducted. Table 5.4 allows the campaign to compare the profiles of all voters, likely voters, and the contacted sample.

Sample Summary of Calling Process and Sample: Calling, Likely Voters, and the Sample

Calling took place June 28 and June 30 and July 1 and July 2, 2002. Computer files of all registrants in counties A and B were obtained, and then all those registrants within the new [number] Assembly district were selected. Each county file records votes for the last six general elections and the year of registration. To focus only on likely voters, an initial sample was drawn that includes only registrants who have voted in at least two of the last six general elections. Two modifications to this selection rule were then made. First, an individual prone to vote may have only recently moved into the area and regis-

tered, so those registering in 2002 were added. Second, some registrants may have voted at least twice, but have moved or ceased to be
active recently. If someone did not vote in the last two general elections, they are unlikely to vote and were deleted.

The number of registrants who completed the survey was 406. The
table below presents the profile of the district, likely voters, and those
we contacted. The composition of the district by party, sex, county,
and age group are shown. The percentages sum down within each
group. For example, within the district, for likely voters, 53.1 percent
are Republican, 16.0 percent are Independents (nonenrolled), and
25.8 percent are Democratic. The profile of those we contacted is
shown in the third column, and the profile of the contacted sample is
very similar to that of likely voters.

Table 5.4   Comparison of All District Registrants, Likely Voters, and Sample

	District	Likely Voters	Sample
Party			
Republican	48.3	53.1	55.2
Independent	20.8	16.0	13.3
Democrat	24.4	25.8	25.1
Sex			
Female	52.7	53.0	54.7
Male	47.3	47.0	45.3
County			
A	51.7	47.3	48.3
B	48.2	52.7	51.7
Age group			
18–29	14.8	4.5	3.7
30–44	29.3	24.3	16.8
45–59	29.2	37.0	38.7
60 plus	26.7	34.3	40.9

Notes

1. It is important to note that this is not the percentage of those within an age
group who voted. It is the percentage of those on the rolls who have a record of
voting in that past year. Registration rolls have enormous turnover, and those
who registered and voted may have left the rolls, and those who were not on the

rolls in any given year may have subsequently registered. The latter group could not have a record of voting. The point is technical, but important, because these figures will differ from figures gathered by the Census, since the Census surveys all people (cite to Census studies), and these figures only indicate the history of those currently on the rolls.

2. For the actual selection, I use a random generating procedure in the SAS software program.

3. Assessing bias in lists of random digit telephone numbers or telephone numbers taken from telephone companies can be very complicated. There is a considerable amount of research that has been done on it, and companies continue to assess this approach as part of the process of convincing their clients that the lists do not have bias. For introductions to this literature, see Groves, et al. 1988 and Brick, et al. 1995.

4. Several web sites provide valuable summaries of the issue of sampling size and margins of error. See www.publicagenda.org/aboutpubopinion/about pubop4.htm; www.pollingreport.com/sampling.htm; www.dssresearch.com/library/general/sampling.asp; www.readexresearch.com/Learn/mse.htm; www.cta.ornl.gov/npts/1995/courseware/Useable_Nav3_18_27.html. One is particularly valuable because it allows you to enter the sample size and it then provides the margin of error for that sample. It is www.columbia.edu/~ssr3/confross.htm.

5. The major concern with individuals in these categories is that they have very different preferences, might actually vote, and will change the results from what the pollster is telling the campaign. There is very little information about these people because it is difficult to obtain an interview with refusals, and in general there is little follow-up. The few studies that have been done indicate that this may not be a serious problem. In terms of demographics, older voters are more likely to refuse, but they are more likely to be at home. Younger voters are less likely to refuse, but less likely to be at home. The result is that these two patterns offset each other, and samples tend to be fairly representative of age groups (Shaiko, et al. 1991). A study that did follow-up nonrespondents found that many do vote, and their voting preferences did not differ from those responding (Bolstein 1991).

6. For the last several years, I have been encountering the situation where during the course of calling, or immediately after we end at 9:00, that someone who is using Caller I.D. calls back to question us about who we are and what the call is about. A few of these people then proceed to say they would like to do the survey.

7. One of the major firms in the business of providing samples for surveys is Survey Sampling Inc. They study nonpublished numbers, refusal rates, and other issues. They publish much of their research on the web page www.worldopinion.com/the_frame/.

Callers and Calling   6

ONE OF THE MOST IMPORTANT MATTERS in the process of calling is conducting it in a way that does not create bias. Bias means that some part of the electorate is over- or underrepresented relative to their actual proportion in the relevant electorate. If a group is underrepresented (e.g., men or Independents) and the group has views different from others in the electorate, their underrepresentation results in inaccurate information.

Callers

To have confidence in the survey's results, it is important to have good callers. The requirements for callers are not demanding, but they are important. Callers need to have a reasonable level of education, the energy to be able to work three to four hours with a sustained focus, the ability to read well, and a friendly style of interacting with respondents. Good callers are invaluable. They work without supervision or prodding and make the process flow along well. Sluggish and ineffective callers who cannot follow the guidelines or who need a lot of breaks slow the process down and require the supervisor to devote time to monitoring the callers. My experience is that it is worthwhile to pay well and get better callers.

The training of callers should be done with care. They need to have the process explained to them and be instructed to not indicate who the survey is for. It is crucial to make sure that they understand the importance of following the script. The essential premise of surveys is that all respondents are presented with exactly the same stimulus (question and set of options) which then allows you to assume (for example) that, faced with a particular set of options, 44 percent chose option A. They also need to be instructed not to interact with the respondent (by strongly agreeing for example) in a way that encourages certain views. I usually brief callers for about thirty minutes on the process by reviewing a guide sheet with them. An example of that guide sheet follows (table 6.1).

Table 6.1   Example: Guidelines to Callers

xxx Assembly District
Caller Guidelines August 5–7, 2002
Purpose of Poll and Source of Sample

- Drew random sample of Republicans in the xxx Assembly District.
- Drew sample from the Board of Election files in Counties A and B.

Calling Process

- If someone asks about "SU" on the Caller ID, say we use a phone bank at SU.
- If respondents express surprise because they have registered to not receive telemarketing calls, explain that you are not selling anything, and this is not a telemarketing call.
- Proceed through name lists from top to bottom, and then repeat progression.
- Deviate from calling names in order only if an individual requests a specific time to be called.

The Call List

You will start with a list of names that look like the one below. You must interview the specific individual listed, not a spouse, friend, or relative. Record the outcome of each call on the "call" lines *using the codes at the end of the list.*

All calls are long distance, so dial 8-1-xxx-# on sheet (wait for beep), then enter code 012345.

Tele	Name	Call 1	Call 2	Reg
3419874	Joe Smith	——	——	X59321

Survey Instructions

1. Be sure to use your name to lend credibility. If registrants want to know who is doing the poll, tell them you do not know who the survey is being done for, but they can call xxx-xxxx during the day to discuss the survey. Assure them of confidentiality. You will experience most refusals right at this point (about 20 percent of all calls

made). The entrance works best if you move directly and quickly into asking questions.

2. PLEASE follow the script at all times; deviations and attempts to elaborate / interpret questions ruin the validity of responses. If the respondent does not know an individual, do not comment or provide additional information. *Also, do not react to comments of the respondent by agreeing or disagreeing.*

3. Please be polite and reread questions if people ask you to do so. Repeat alternatives when necessary.

Types of Responses and Coding on the Call List

Each name on your list will result in an outcome of one of three types. Please classify each name into one of the following types and record the outcome on the list of names.

1. Completion: Respondent completes survey. *Record all responses on the survey and CMP on list of names.* When you obtain a completion, record at the top:

- The registration number (reg) of the respondent.
- The name of the individual contacted.
- Your initials, so we can ask you about unclear recordings.

The registration number and name must be there or we won't be able to find the individual in the data file.

2. Failures (to be eliminated): For each of these write the appropriate code shown below and put a line through the name with the red pen.
    REF   Refusals
    UNR   Unreachable: definitely out of area for the evening. Write the situation under response and also cross out. Be sure to ask about Tuesday or Wednesday.
    BN   Bad number: disconnected, fax, or business number, moved, no longer at number, etc. Indicate the problem, and cross out the name.

3. Retrys: for each of these write RETRY.
    No-answer: No answer, busy, answering machine.
    Not available currently, but possibly Tuesday or Wednesday.
    Do not pursue changed numbers. We do not know where they are.

Campaigns sometimes try to reduce the costs of polling by hiring a pollster and promising to recruit campaign volunteers to do the calling. Volunteers are a pollster's nightmare. They often show up later than necessary, requiring the supervisor to repeat the explanation of the process to be followed. This is very distracting to the supervisor. Many also presume they can leave at any time to attend to personal matters, resulting in phones being unused. They cannot always be expected to follow the script. It is best to *refuse* any efforts by a campaign to use volunteers. Multiple problems result, and it undermines the credibility of the results. Callers should be people who are paid, with the expectation that they will work full-time during the times set for calling. It is important to have energetic and articulate people who can work for three to four hours without much difficulty. College students and adults who want a part-time job are very good for this kind of work.

Interviewer Effects

Even after taking considerable care to avoid bias by carefully reviewing the questions and the language and by carefully drawing a sample, there are circumstances in which the callers can unknowingly create bias. In situations when the campaign involves gender and race issues—either in the questions or the candidates, or both—the gender and race of the callers can affect the responses of voters and produce results that are inaccurate.

The general pattern is that the race or sex of a caller may influence the response to a question if the question involves issues of race or sex. Respondents answer differently if a caller is female and the questions are about issues involving females. Respondents answer differently if the caller is recognizably black or Latino and the questions involve issues affecting minorities or one of the candidates is a minority. If a question is asked about whether there should be more equality in pay rates for women and the caller is a female, the respondent is more likely to respond yes to a female caller than to a male caller. If the respondent is also female, the percentage will be even higher (Kane and Macaulay 1993, 10–19). If a question is asked about whether more should be done to ensure equality of treatment for minorities in hiring, the responses will be different if the caller is heard as having black or Latino speech patterns (Finkel, et al. 1991, 317–18). In cases where one candidate is white and the other is a minority, the effect is likely to be that white respondents will be more likely to tell a minority caller that they will vote for the minority and minority respondents will probably be more likely to indicate to a minority caller that they will vote for the minority candidate. A white respondent may be more inclined to tell a white caller that she will vote for the white candidate.

The important matter is to be aware of possible interviewer effects. If a race involves a female and a male and issues of the treatment of women play a role, it is important to have a set of callers that is balanced by sex to try to reduce the effects of the sex of the caller and the interaction of the two. It may be valuable to include a code as to the sex of the caller and enter it with each survey result and then check to see if the results vary by the sex of the caller or if any interaction effects occur. If a district is racially diverse, then it is important to have a diverse set of callers and to run the same check for interviewer or interaction effects.

Cycling Through Lists

The goal of the calling process is to preserve the randomness of the initial sample. There are two essential ways to do this. Academic surveys generally draw a fairly limited sample, and then to ensure that everyone on the list has a chance to be included in the survey, the callers engage in repeated callbacks scattered across the day to maximize the possibility of contacting everyone on the list. This is a process that can be lengthy (spread over several weeks) and expensive, because of the need to have a set of callers who repeatedly call the individuals not yet reached. This process is absolutely appropriate if an organization has the time and money to pursue this approach. Like pretesting, however, it is a process that most campaigns cannot afford and do not have the time to follow. Further, evidence indicates that the results from a more condensed process with fewer callbacks do not differ from those obtained from a more drawn out process with many attempts to reach potential respondents (Keeter, et al. 2000).

The alternative to the repeated callback approach, as discussed in chapter 5, is to pull a list much larger than the desired sample and cycle through it in a random fashion over a few days. Each noncontacted number may receive only two calls. If the list is sorted by last name, then there is no bias to the list, and having one caller who is more successful than another does not cause problems.

Calling should ideally be done at all times of the day, to make sure that those who work in the evening have a chance to participate. Again, campaigns usually cannot afford to do that, and most calls are made in the evening, from 5:30 to 9:00. One way to minimize the problems of missing people because of work schedules is to call on Saturday and Sunday afternoons and evenings. On Sunday nights it is not a good idea to call after 8:00 p.m., because people become irritated by late calls on Sunday. It is best to avoid nights when there is a major local or national sports event on television.

The Crucial Part: Analysis and Developing a Campaign Plan

O NCE THE SCRIPT HAS BEEN WRITTEN and the calls made, the most important matter is analyzing and interpreting the results for the campaign. With benchmark polls it is crucial to provide an overall interpretation that will lead to a plan. With tracking polls it is important to provide a sense of trends, what is working and what is not working. The job of the analyst is to review the results, interpret them, and reduce the data to a narrative that can be put together in a report with recommendations for action. It does the campaign no good to inundate it with too much information. The campaign needs to know what to focus on, and the report has to provide that advice.

The goal in constructing an analysis is to figure out what the candidate and campaign need to do to win. Candidates and campaign managers are interested in the relationships among responses, much as an academic is, but only with a concern for how those relationships tell them what must be done to maintain a lead or to develop one. As one campaign manager said, amidst a debate about whether to conduct a benchmark poll: "A polling report is like a roadmap. I know where I want to go, but without a roadmap I don't know how to get there." Running for office is very demanding and consuming, and candidates want a poll to tell them what they need to do to win the election.

Techniques of Analysis

The analytical techniques are relatively simple. The basic approach is to analyze frequencies and crosstabs. The first example (table 7.1) presents the frequency results for a question. The second table presents an example of a crosstab that statistical software programs will generate.

resent the number of respondents who choose each the percentage that choose each category. The follow-□ example of such results. These results provide the basic information of the distribution of candidate support or support for policy positions.

Table 7.1   Example of Frequencies

Q 5. This November Sue Smith, the Democrat, will run against Joe Jones, the Republican, for the local Assembly seat. Would you most likely vote for Smith or Jones? *(If a choice was made, ask: Would that be definitely Smith / Jones or just probably Smith / Jones?)*

	Number	Percent
Definitely Smith	83	27.7
Probably Smith	56	18.5
Probably Jones	38	12.8
Definitely Jones	41	13.6
No choice	82	27.4

Crosstabs

The other important way of assessing results is crosstabs. A crosstab presents information on how people with one response to a question are distributed on another question. In requesting crosstabs, the practice is to choose that issue that is probably causal (response A) to run along the left and that which is presumably affected (response B) to run along the top. A respondent trait like party registration, sex, or area of residence is relatively unchanging and is not caused by support for the candidate, so it is treated as causal and goes along the left. Opinions on abortion or taxes are relatively set and are not caused by support for the candidate, so they go along the left. The vote choice goes along the top. This arraying of the data allows the pollster to assess whether respondents who are Republicans differ in their candidate or policy support from those who are Democrats. A crosstab follows and provides the information that is used in analyses. The results and what they indicate are as follows (table 7.2).

Actual numbers of respondents: The first number in each cell is the number of respondents who are in a category along the left and a category along the top. They meet two conditions. In this case it is the actual number of respondents who are registered in one party and support a candidate or have no choice. In the first cell there are thirty-three respondents who are Republican and support the Democratic candidate.

Row percents: The second number in the cell is the row percent, or the distribution of candidate choices among those who are Republican. The row percents and comparison of them are usually the most important concern in reviewing tables. They provide an indication of differences in reaction by group.

Table 7.2   Crosstab of Party Enrollment and Vote Choice

	D Candidate	R Candidate	Undecided	Totals
Republican	33	60	27	120
	27.3	50.0	22.5	40.0
	27.3	58.8	35.1	
Independent	25	19	23	67
	37.3	28.4	34.3	22.3
	20.7	18.6	29.9	
Democrat	61	17	24	102
	59.8	16.7	23.5	34.0
	50.4	16.7	31.2	
Other	2	6	3	11
	18.2	54.5	27.3	3.6
	1.7	5.9	3.9	
Total	121	102	77	300
	40.3	34.0	25.7	100.0

Column percents: The third number is the column percent, which indicates how those who support the Democratic candidate are distributed by party registration. Column percents can be compared to assess the relative source of support for a candidate or position and how the sources of support vary.

Margin totals and percents for the response running across the top: The numbers at the very bottom, also known as "marginals," indicate the overall support for a candidate or position. They are obviously of fundamental importance to indicate the overall distribution of support for the candidates or an issue position.

Margin totals and percents for the response running down the left: The numbers to the right, again known as the "marginals," are valuable to indicate what percentage of all respondents are in the categories shown to the left. These percentages are important to indicate the composition of the district. These percentages provide a check on reading too much into a specific row percentage. A candidate might do well among a particular group (Other Party registrants), and the candidate might be encouraged that he is appealing to those dissatisfied with the status quo. The reality, however, is that only 3.6 percent of all respondents are in this category. Focusing on this group will provide little electoral payoff, so the group should receive limited attention.

Candidate Visibility and Voter Reactions

Once the crosstabs are available, the first concern of a campaign is the general visibility and rating of its candidate and how this compares with the opponent. The initial focus is always on name recognition and the matchup. If one candidate is an incumbent, the questions on job approval and reelection support are also very important. Open-seat races and those involving an incumbent are very different, so they are discussed separately below.

In making assessments of candidates, some campaigns "laws" are crucial. The paramount rule is that all campaigns are different. Each campaign has a candidate with a different personality, different abilities to raise money, and different sets of issues. The challenge is to use the polling information to find that combination of partisan appeals and issue positions that will help the candidate win. The other crucial matter is that all politics is conditional. No formula can be applied to assessing a campaign. Not all Republicans can focus on tax cuts and crime. Not all Democrats focus on social programs. It is crucial to take into account the conditions of each election (is it a high- or low-turnout race, is one candidate better known, how does the partisan distribution differ, and what issues are significant and how do they divide the electorate and provide a potential electoral base for the candidate?).

Any analysis should begin with the name recognition of candidates. As noted earlier, most voters do not follow politics closely, and for most candidates the biggest challenge they face is building up their visibility. The initial examples focus on open-seat races and involve varying situations common for those entering open-seat contests. Each situation prompts a concern for different kinds of information. Then races in which an incumbent is present are examined.

Open-Seat Contests

The first situation (candidates A in table 7.3) involves a race in which both candidates, each of whom may have been elected to a lower-level office, are relatively unknown. Over 50 percent have never heard of them and another 20 percent have no specific impression (no opinion) of them. Many candidates entering open-seats races have high percentages of voters who have never heard of them. This often surprises them, since they move in a world where everyone they know knows them. It is important to tell them at this point that these results are typical. This information indicates that the race could be wide open, since neither is very well known.

Faced with these results, the next issue is what scenarios might develop as the campaign evolves. Assuming that the candidate can raise money and increase his visibility, the important matter is the partisan makeup of the district. Most partisans (those registered in or identifying with a party) vote for the candidate of their party (Bartells 2000). If a candidate is running in a district in which a majority of voters are registered in her party, then she might assume, with a well-run campaign and a message compatible with the district, that she will be able to bring her partisans "home" and she has a good chance of winning the election. If a candidate is in a situation where his partisans are only 30–40 percent of the district, then he has to analyze issues with a focus on how to create crossover votes (defections from the other party to him). Otherwise, he has to try to raise much more money than the other candidate and create higher name recognition and ratings than his opponent.

In cases of low name recognition for both candidates, the initial results can be discouraging, but they can also be useful for raising money. The name recognition and ratings numbers indicate that the candidate has a long way to go. To show this to campaign workers can be discouraging, because they may be worried about devoting long hours to someone with such little visibility. Most campaigns do not share such numbers. On the other hand, these numbers can be presented to potential contributors to show them that it is anyone's race (depending on party registration in the jurisdiction) and that their money can be very valuable. How information can be presented to help a candidate raise money is discussed below.

Table 7.3   Variations in Name Recognition—Open Seat

Q. Next, I'd like to read you the names of some people who have been in the news recently. For each name, could you please tell me whether your impressions of that person are favorable or unfavorable. If you have never heard of someone, or don't know enough to rate the person, just say so.

	Favorable	Unfavorable	No Opinion	Never Heard Of
Democrat A	19.5	4.6	23.7	52.2
Republican A	22.4	5.2	21.4	51.0
Democrat B	42.6	7.2	18.5	31.7
Republican B	11.3	2.2	17.5	69.0
Democrat C	41.2	24.5	11.1	23.2
Republican C	16.4	2.7	19.1	61.8

The second situation (candidates B in table 7.3) represents a case where one candidate is much better known (the Democrat), and the Republican has to spend considerable money to catch up to her opponent in name recognition. In this case, the Democrat might want to use these results and those from the matchup to present to contributors to convince them that he is the likely winner and that a contribution will not be wasted on a losing effort. The Republican, on the other hand, has to raise money and find some issues in the poll results that will provide a means to critique the Democrat.

The third situation (candidates C in table 7.3) represents a variation on the second situation, but with more hope for the Republican. The Democrat is much better known but has acquired some "negatives" (unfavorable ratings) among the public. While the Republican is less well known, he begins with the knowledge that his opponent has created some negative reactions among the electorate. Candidates very often end up with negatives in the high-twenty or low-thirty percentages at the end of a campaign, after all the attacks, but it is a sign of a potential problem when a candidate begins with negatives in the mid-twenty percentages.

Incumbent Contests

Contests with an incumbent are different, largely because the incumbent has developed more of a presence and image among the electorate and because there is more information that can be gathered about an incumbent. The following example (table 7.4) presents two incumbents facing challengers. The first represents a relatively strong incumbent and a weak challenger. The second represents a potentially vulnerable incumbent.

The first situation represents a very common situation when a challenger decides to take on an incumbent. The incumbent not only has fairly good name recognition and ratings, but the ratings are also good among Independents and those registered in the opposite party. The incumbent has been able through the cumulative impact of his actions to create a very positive image and one that even those in the opposite party find acceptable. The Republican challenger does not face the possibility that the incumbent has a base primarily in her own party and is weak outside that base. The challenger is not well known, and convincing contributors and workers that the incumbent can be beaten will be difficult.

In addition to the basic information on name recognition, there is the issue of job approval and reelection support. If both of these are in the 50–60 percent range and fairly uniform across party registration groups, it will be difficult to find a base to appeal to, to build momentum in a campaign. A majority wants to reelect the incumbent, and the challenger faces the task of not only building up name recognition but also presenting a case for why the incumbent should not be reelected. That takes more money and time, and it may not be possible for a challenger to raise much money if potential contributors see an incumbent with high name recognition, very good ratings, and job approval and reelection percentages above 55.

Many times the incumbent does not find that all these numbers are high. It is not uncommon that an incumbent, who is in her first term, takes a poll a year away from the next race and has good name recogni-

Table 7.4   Variations in Name Recognition—Incumbent Present

	Reaction to Candidates			
	Favorable	Unfavorable	No Opinion	Never Heard Of
Seat A—Democratic Incumbent	55.8	11.3	13.5	19.4
Democrats	64.7	7.2	10.1	18.0
Independents	54.3	8.4	15.7	21.6
Republicans	49.5	12.0	12.2	26.3
Seat A—Republican Challenger	16.6	5.1	29.1	49.2
Democrats	4.5	2.4	6.3	86.8
Independents	9.8	3.7	10.9	75.6
Republicans	22.5	3.9	17.9	55.7
Seat B—Democratic Challenger	29.4	7.8	18.5	44.3
Democrats	54.6	8.9	14.5	22.0
Independents	21.0	6.6	33.7	38.7
Republicans	14.6	2.2	40.0	43.2
Seat B—Republican Incumbent	53.2	32.7	7.0	7.1
Democrats	22.6	41.4	10.2	25.8
Independents	33.5	23.1	8.8	34.6
Republicans	69.7	16.7	9.2	4.4

tion and good ratings, but the job approval and reelection numbers are below 50 percent. This is a sign that the electorate views the incumbent favorably, but may not really know much about what the incumbent has done. Indeed, it may be valuable in such situations to ask the job approval question "Do you approve or disapprove of the job x is doing as y, or don't you know enough to judge that?" This, rather than pushing respondents to make a choice, gives respondents the option of indicating their lack of awareness of just what the public official has accomplished. In many situations where a public official, and particularly executives such as mayors, county executives, and district attorneys, is in the newspapers a lot and respondents may not recall anything negative about the individual. They have a favorable impression of the person and are inclined to say they approve of his job performance but do not really know what he has done. It is important for the campaign to draw that information out. Otherwise, the incumbent and his campaign staff may presume they are in a strong situation and do not need to conduct a campaign explaining what he has accomplished. In this situation a challenger may conduct a poll and find that the incumbent's support is "soft" (reelection support is 40–45 percent) and that a challenge can be mounted. For the incumbent this means that, even with good name identification and ratings and without a declared opponent, it is still necessary to raise money and plan a campaign. Potential contributors often find this a puzzling situation, and it may be unwise to explain that there is a potential vulnerability, as that word can spread.

The second situation shown in table 7.4 (B) is more troubling for an incumbent and enticing for a challenger. The incumbent has fairly high negatives, and he polarizes partisans. Negatives over 30 percent usually represent a sign of problems with the incumbent's image. Ratings that decline markedly from his party to the other also indicate that there is a potential base for a challenger. If the job approval and reelection support numbers are below 50 percent, with the same divisions shown for ratings, then there is a possibility that a challenger can beat this incumbent. It is necessary to take these poll results to the party leaders and get them to help her raise money to build her name recognition.

For incumbents, situation B presents a problem that has to be addressed. The decisions about what to do vary considerably by the situation a candidate is in. The campaigns of two U.S. Senate elections illustrate this. In February 1998 Republican Al D'Amato (N.Y.) was running for his fourth term in the Senate, against Democrat Chuck Schumer, a sitting member of the House of Representatives. D'Amato's ratings were 36 percent favorable and 35 percent unfavorable, with 8 percent having never heard of him. After eighteen years in office he was fairly well known and well defined. That is, a substantial percentage of voters had an image of him, and it was a decidedly mixed assessment. Schumer's image, as a New York City congressman, was much less formed statewide. His ratings were 23 percent favorable to 10 percent unfavorable, with 58 percent having never heard of him.[1] D'Amato knew that it would be difficult to change his image in a short period of time. Faced with poll results showing his bad ratio of favorable to unfavorable reactions, and having an opponent with a relatively unformed image, D'Amato chose to accept where he was and focus on "defining" his opponent. That is, he chose to try to tell voters who Chuck Schumer was, so that Chuck Schumer would not be able to present and define himself. His strategy did result in raising Schumer's negatives, and by the end of the race, Schumer was at 37 percent favorable to 28 percent unfavorable. Schumer, in response, was not timid, and he focused on attacking D'Amato and making sure his negatives stayed high. That strategy worked, and by the end of the election, D'Amato was at 35 percent favorable to 43 percent unfavorable, and Schumer won a close race.

If a candidate is not as well defined, she may choose a different route. In March 2000, Hillary Clinton was just beginning her campaign for the U.S. Senate seat in New York. Her ratings in March and April were essentially 35 percent favorable and 35 percent unfavorable. She apparently believed that she could soften the negative image she had developed in the several years prior to 2000, and much of her early campaigning was devoted to a "listening tour" of the state to present herself anew to the voters. She ran positive ads on television and went from county to county attending relatively low-key events where she talked with people about state issues. While her opponent ran numerous negative ads about her, it appeared that her approach did restrain the development of a more negative image, and by the end of the campaign, her ratings were 45 percent favorable with 34 percent unfavorable, and she won the election.

All these situations differ, and the role of polling is to provide basic information about the visibility of and reaction to a candidate. It is then the job of the pollster and the campaign staff to consider the larger context—the likely actions of the opponent and the likely dynamics of the campaign—and decide on a plan for the campaign. This plan may have to change as the campaign develops, as will be discussed below, but a campaign plan starts with the basic information just reviewed.

The Matchup Information

Name recognition and ratings are essential information, but the important matter is how people indicate they will vote. The first thing to communicate to candidates is that the results are not a prediction. They are truly just a portrait of where the race is at that moment. Each campaign will respond to the results with a plan about how to either maintain or change them. If the results are early in the campaign, most people are not paying much attention to the candidates, even at the presidential level (Patterson 2002). The combination of campaign efforts, and greater media and electoral attention as the campaign proceeds, will change the results. No candidate should be too reassured or too discouraged by early results. They define where things are and indicate what must be done.

Benchmark polls.

The next step in the analysis is to assess the nature of support by party. The best indicator of whether someone can be mobilized for a candidate or her opponent is the voter's partisan identification. Voters develop party attachments over time, and they reflect and guide much of their reaction to the political world (Flanigan and Zingale 2001). Those with a partisan identity generally vote for their candidate, but that is at the end of a campaign after persistent efforts to influence voters (Bartells 2000). In the early stages of a campaign, the crosstab of party by matchup indicates where a candidate stands with her party and with other voters whose support she may need to win, or at least do reasonably well among. The crosstabs indicate, as of that point in the campaign, whether the candidate is winning her base or needs to build that support and how she is doing among Independents and the opposition party.

There are several general things to look for. The first matter is the distribution of party registration in the district, or the marginals. Does it provide a sufficient base for one candidate to win, if that electoral base can be mobilized? Or, does the candidate have to attract cross-over voters to have a chance to put together a majority? What is the general relationship between name recognition and support? If matchup support is greater than name recognition levels, it may indicate that the tendency is for partisan voting to be strong and the candidate can count on a partisan vote. It could also indicate superficial support for a candidate, based on just hearing the individual is a Republican or a Democrat. If matchup support is much less than name recognition, it could mean that partisan attachments are fairly weak or that the candidate has not been able, as of this point, to create much sense of who he is, so that voters are not yet ready to support the candidate of their party.

The next concern is the pattern of partisan attachments and candidate choice. A considerable variety of situations can occur, and a few of the more typical are discussed here. For each situation, vote choice by party registration is presented along with the percentage of the district (likely voters) in each party. In these cases, it is presumed that an incumbent is running against a fairly well-known challenger. Many challengers are not well known in the beginning, and incumbents are faced with the situation of waiting to see how the challenger's visibility increases. It is assumed that a well-known challenger has decided to enter the race, to indicate how a strategy might evolve in such a situation.

Situation A (table 7.5) is fairly typical of a competitive district. The incumbent is a Democrat. Party registration is evenly balanced, and each candidate does well within her party base. Those who are partisan are more likely to follow politics and to be inclined to make a choice. Independents typically follow politics less and are not as likely to have made a choice early in a campaign. The incumbent does well among Democrats and fairly well among Independents, while the challenger does well within her own party. In this case, each candidate faces two challenges. Each must make sure she connects with her core base of partisans and mobilizes them to vote. The partisans are of adequate numbers to provide much of a base for winning the election. Each candidate also faces the challenge of finding a way to build name recognition and support among Independents. The outcome will hinge on who can mobilize her base and who can find a message that attracts Independents and gets them to vote.

The second situation (B) presents a very different problem for the candidate. The incumbent is a Democrat and does well among Democrats and Independents. The challenger, less well known, is losing his own party. The challenger faces the need to concentrate on his own party and be able to pull his partisan supporters away from the incumbent. Given that partisans are prone to vote for a candidate from their own party, mobilizing Republican support should be very possible, but it is essential to concentrate on this and change these percentages. If efforts are not made to change this situation quickly, the incumbent's polls will indicate that the challenger is not doing well, which will inhibit people from contributing money and feeling enthusiastic.

The final situation (C) represents one very common in many political districts. Most districts do not begin with a balanced partisan composition. In this case a Republican incumbent is in a district that is 50 percent Republican, and he has very strong support within his own party. Independents are again less inclined to have made a choice. The primary goal of the incumbent is to maintain support within his own party and do as much as possible to build reasonable support among Independents. That combination should produce a victory. The challenger faces a difficult but very common situation. Only 25 percent of the district is Democratic. While he does well among his partisan base, it is not sufficient to win the race. His strategy must be to find a way to

Table 7.5   Vote Choice by Party Registration

	Candidate Choices		
	Democrat	Republican	No Opinion
Situation A			
Party (and % of district)			
Republican (40)	18.7	59.4	21.9
Independent (15)	37.6	25.6	36.8
Democrat (40)	62.9	11.3	25.8
Situation B			
Party (and % of district)			
Republican (40)	27.7	46.6	25.7
Independent (15)	46.5	25.6	27.9
Democrat (40)	62.9	8.6	28.5
Situation C			
Party (and % of district)			
Republican (50)	11.5	73.2	15.3
Independent (15)	25.7	21.0	53.3
Democrat (25)	62.9	8.6	28.5

Note: The percentages for partisan composition of the district do not sum to 100 because some registrants may choose a third party and third parties are not included here.

appeal to Independents and reduce the incumbent's support among Republicans. Faced with this situation, he must find some issues that will provide a means to move voters away from the incumbent.

Using Information to Seek Support

Initial polls indicate where candidates are and what they need to do to win. They may be winning or losing. Particularly when a candidate is losing, it is important to try to present the candidate's prospects in a positive light to convince potential supporters and contributors to support the campaign. A common approach in these situations is to reorganize the data as in the following example (table 7.6). The goal is to assess the extent to which the candidate's problem is just not being well known. If that is the primary problem, it is possible to make the argument to contributors that with more money they have a serious chance to win the election. Contributors are reluctant to donate money to a campaign that is likely to fail, so they need information that there is a possibility.

The results are created by recoding the name recognition data.

Those respondents who have some impression of a candidate—either favorable or unfavorable—are classified as knowing the candidate. Those who choose "no opinion" or "never heard of" are classified as don't know the candidate. The matchup results are then sorted by "know" and "don't know" for each candidate. The results indicate how well the candidate does in the situation where both are known and the differentials in name recognition that the candidate faces. Table 7.6 presents these results for two campaigns in their early stages.

Table 7.6   The Role of Name Recognition

Situation A	Matchup Choices			
	Democrat	Republican	No Choice	Percent Sample
Know both	33.3	33.3	33.3	10.6
Know D, not R	65.1	9.4	25.5	46.9
Know R, not D	16.7	50.0	33.3	2.7
Don't know either	23.6	22.5	53.9	39.8
Overall matchup	44.0	18.2	37.8	100
Situation B	Democrat	Republican	No Choice	Percent Sample
Know both	42.9	42.9	14.3	9.5
Know D, not R	72.4	3.5	24.1	13.1
Know R, not D	3.1	84.4	12.5	14.4
Don't know either	37.9	17.7	44.3	63.1
Overall matchup	37.8	27.9	34.2	100

In situation A, when both are known (10.6 percent of the sample), the matchup is even at 33.3 percent versus 33.3 percent. While that is encouraging, the difficulty the Republican faces is that 46.9 percent know the Democrat only and 2.7 percent know just the Republican. The difference in name recognition is enormous, and the candidate, despite many positive comments about her energy and presence, will have a difficult time convincing party leaders that she has a chance. In situation B, the matchup is again even among those who know both candidates, but it is again the case that only a small percentage (9.5) of the entire sample knows both. The Democratic incumbent had been in office only two years and had not used the time to build her name recognition. The result was that she began the campaign for re-election with no great advantage in name recognition. Of the sample, 13.1 percent knew only the Democrat and 14.4 percent knew only the Republican. The matchup was also reasonably close, with the incumbent winning by only 10 percentage points. In this case, a well-

charismatic,

organized Republican candidate was able to convince party leaders that he had a chance to win the race. The Republican Party leaders raised money and urged others to do the same, informing potential contributors that the candidate had a chance to win. The Democrat eventually won in a close race.

The pollster is very often asked to prepare a one- to two-page memo with this kind of information, which can then be presented to potential supporters. The memo will use only limited amounts of information. The memo cannot misrepresent information, since some in the campaign will see or know about the full poll report and will react to misrepresentation. But it is possible to present a summary table like the one just reviewed and use it in situation B to try to persuade contributors to help out. This information will be of greater value if the candidate has a record of being energetic and organized and is seen as personable by others. If those conditions are not present, supporters and contributors are likely to listen but hold back in making significant commitments to the campaign.

The Role of Issues

While much of campaign activity focuses on building up name recognition and visibility for the candidate, issues are the raw material of building a connection with voters. It is one thing to build up candidate visibility, but then there has to be a reason to get people to want to vote for the candidate. While many people think that political campaigns have become beauty contests, with positive and negative images of candidates the primary message, issues are the route to building up any depth of support for a candidate after voters know a candidate exists.

Even candidates sometimes downplay the role of issues. I frequently find that new candidates, or candidates moving up an office level, presume that campaigns are visibility and credentials races. That is, they think that the contest is really about who is most qualified. In meetings these candidates will continually stress that they have more experience or better credentials than their opponent. They want to include many questions that present the differences in credentials and then ask who is most qualified, or whether this difference makes the respondent more likely to vote for x or y. Credentials may be enough, particularly in a jurisdiction where one party dominates, but in most cases they do not motivate voters sufficiently to mobilize partisans to support a candidate. The crosstabs do not indicate that differences in credentials create significant differences in voting inclinations. Partisans hold attachments to a party for many reasons, but issue differences are generally important to them. Issues become the way to mobilize predisposed partisans or to encourage partisans to defect from voting for their own candidate.

The way in which issues are used varies with the partisan composition of the district. If a candidate is running in a district where her party is the majority, the challenge is to mobilize that base. She must create party voting. If a candidate begins with a majority of partisans, and she largely shares the beliefs of her party, the challenge is one of having the resources to articulate her compatibility.

If a candidate is running in a district where his party is in the minority, his challenge is to find a way to move voters away from voting for the candidate of their party. He must create defections from party voting. Issues are the means by which candidates can build or diminish party loyalty. The challenge is to find issues that will draw voters away and then devise a plan to do that.

To begin to understand the role of issues in a jurisdiction, it is essential to conduct a thorough analysis of issues, asking the following questions.

ISSUE ANALYSIS QUESTIONS

- What is the distribution of opinion on issues within the district? Is there a consensus within the district about significant issues, or is there a division of opinion?
- How do the candidate's positions coincide with the views of voters? Are there positions the candidate holds that she should stress because a majority agree with her position? Are there issues she should deemphasize because a majority disagrees with her?
- Are issue positions related to each other, so that they reinforce each other? That is, are conservatives consistent across several issues, so that appeals on one issue are likely to affect connections on other issues?
- To what extent do issues provide a basis of support for the candidate and is that basis coherent? That is, if the candidate is liberal, do those with liberal views strongly support him, or is it necessary for the campaign to build that connection?
- Do some issues currently have greater impact in moving voters

than others? Is that because some issues have greater saliency or are more visible and important to voters, or because a candidate is identified with an issue that has been prominent?

- Are there issues which might provide a basis for moving voters? Are there issues that divide the electorate, but positions on these issues do not connect voters in any way to candidates? If the candidate supports specific views, can the campaign identify the candidate's position and bring voters supporting that position to the candidate?

The Distribution of Opinion and the Candidate's Positions

The first thing that any campaign should assess regarding issues is the distribution of opinion within the jurisdiction. The results will not, of course, include all issues but only those the campaign chose to ask about because the candidate and campaign manager think these issues will be important. These distributions are examined by reviewing the frequencies of responses for each question.

The next concern is whether the candidate's views are in sync with the district. Does the candidate advocate positions that are supported or not supported by a majority of the electorate? For example, if a candidate is running for county executive in a county facing a significant deficit and the candidate favors cutting services as an answer, does a majority of likely voters also support this? If so, the candidate probably faces no problem in making his position widely known. In this case, however, there is the question of how voters will react once cuts in specific services—parks, police, and funding for schools—are announced. If the candidate supports cuts in services, a poll should include specific questions as to which services to see if the abstract support for cutting services is matched by support for cuts in specific areas.

On other issues, a candidate may face a situation where his views are contrary to the majority. The same conservative who favors budget cuts may be pro-life and running in a county where a majority of the district is pro-choice. There are several ways to respond to this situation. If the opponent is also pro-life, then the issue will not play a role in vote choices and can be ignored. If the opponent is pro-choice and this issue is not a relevant county issue because the county may not be

[handwritten: if no relevance]

in a position to affect public policy in this area, then the best approach may be to note the issue has no relevance for this race and ignore it.

If the issue is relevant because a candidate is running for the state legislature or Congress, where a vote on a bill related to abortion or choice could occur, then it may not be possible to ignore the issue. How much it becomes an issue will depend on the opponent and his position and press coverage. Many people assume that when a candidate holds a position in opposition to a majority of the district, polling will lead the candidate to change his position. A typical comment is "Candidates poll to find out what their positions are or should be on issues—the same way toothpaste companies poll to find features customers might pay for" (Ross 2000). Despite this popular impression, polling does not lead to the conclusion that the candidate should change his views but that he should deemphasize some issues and stress others as much as possible. The goal is to find what to call attention to during a campaign and what to try to avoid. While polling is widely discussed as if candidates begin with no positions and then decide what to believe dependent on the poll results, this is rarely the case. If a candidate already has a publicly announced position, changing his views will likely result in charges by the opponent that the candidate is changing his views, is without any character, and cannot be trusted in the future. If a candidate does change his views, it is likely to do more damage than good because the press will report the change and suggest it is opportunistic, which will hurt the candidate. Further, a change from a pro-life to pro-choice position may not gain any supporters. Those who are pro-life may be so alienated by the change that it reduces support from them, even though these voters have no candidate to vote for who supports their views. Those who are pro-choice may be suspicious of the newly "converted" candidate and uneasy about supporting him. There is generally little to gain from taking a poll and changing an opinion.

There are occasions, however, when politicians have no clear positions and polls provide information about public opinion as issues emerge. During 2002 there was a continual series of stories about corporate financial scandals involving CEOs who were accused of manipulating accounting practices to make profits look greater than they were. The argument was that they did this because their compensation was in the form of the right to buy company stock at a set price. If profits were higher, stock prices would increase, and CEOs could buy stock at, say, $10 a share, even though its value on the market had increased to $25 a share. They could then sell the stock and pocket the difference, before they had to reveal that profits were not as great as reported. In early 2002 this was not a major public issue, and few members of Congress had a public position, since the issue had so little visibility. The issue of whether to require more corporate disclosure quickly became more prominent, with polls showing an abrupt rise in distrust of business during the summer of 2002 (Horovitz 2002, 1). Republicans were already much less inclined than Democrats to impose more regulations on business, and few had taken strong stands on specific aspects of the issue because it had not been prominent. Faced with growing concern about the issue, many congressional Republicans were willing to adopt a position favoring more regulation. In this case of an emerging public concern about an issue, Republican Party members were willing to ease their generally supportive position of business and vote for more regulations. Public officials can adapt as issues emerge, but it is rare for them to change specific positions.

To return to an issue like abortion, there are two other responses that a candidate with a position contrary to the majority can make, and polling is again valuable for deciding how to respond. The first response is to see if opinion is not as simple as it might seem and if there is room for a candidate position that might reduce the impact of the issue on voting. While the general practice is to push respondents into the categories of pro-life and pro-choice to get an idea of the divisions of opinion that exist, it may be worthwhile to probe more to see if the divisions are not so simple and if there is language that a candidate can use that captures that greater complexity and allows the candidate to appeal to more voters. A candidate might be opposed to abortion but willing to allow it in cases of rape, incest, or a severely deformed fetus. The standard question about abortion is the first one shown in table 7.7. A candidate might ask that the second question be presented instead, to determine if there is more variation. If there are significant percentages choosing the second and third choices, then the candidate could focus on presenting that position and worry less about its generating opposition.

If a candidate is not in favor of exceptions, then it is still be possible to assess whether there is some ambivalence among voters that a candidate might to appeal to. The third question indicates another possi-

Table 7.7   Probing an Issue

Q. Do you generally regard yourself as pro-choice or pro-life?
   1 ___ pro-choice   2 ___ pro-life   3 ___ no opinion

Q. On the issue of abortion, which of the following best describes your position?
   1 ___ I am opposed to abortion in all circumstances.
   2 ___ I am opposed to abortion except for situations of rape or incest.
   3 ___ I am opposed to abortion except for situations of rape, incest, and a deformed fetus.
   4 ___ I support the right to abortion.

Q. On the issue of abortion, which of the following best describes your position?
   1 ___ I am pro-life, or opposed to abortion.
   2 ___ I am pro-choice, or in favor of women making their own choice, but worry about too many abortions occurring.
   3 ___ I am pro-choice, or in favor of women making their own choice.

Q. On the issue of government providing help for _____,
   1 ___ I am opposed.
   2 ___ I support it, but worry about the size of the tax breaks being given.
   3 ___ I support it.

ble way to ask about the issue. If a substantial percentage chooses the middle option, so that a majority chooses pro-life or that they are pro-choice but worry about too many abortions, then a candidate can, if questioned, acknowledge his opposition to abortion, but primarily stress his concern about too many abortions. The response might appeal to those who do have this worry, and these voters may see the candidate less as an ideologue than as someone with concerns they share. The hoped for result is that this issue will be less divisive and it will have less impact on vote choices.

This same approach can be applied to other issues. Many times a candidate is faced with an issue about some major local project. Local communities are increasingly faced with proposals from large businesses—manufacturing firms, shopping malls, sports stadiums, hotel and convention complexes—that promise many local jobs but want large tax breaks or subsidies of loans. A candidate might support the local project because of the economic development it will bring but worry about community opposition. The question in a poll might be "do you support or oppose _____?" But it also could be something like the last question in table 7.7. If the middle category is chosen by a large percentage, then the candidate can support the project but urge that the negotiators be tough in demanding some guarantees for the community. *Find a middle ground.*

Finally, it may simply be the case that the candidate is on the wrong side of the issue, with no way to soften the difference from the majority. If so, it is important to see how important the issue is to voters. There are two ways to assess this. One is to present voters with a set of issues and ask them which is most important in their voting decision. If an issue is not among the most important, it may be possible for a candidate, when asked about the issue, to simply state his or her views and hope that it is not central to most voters. The other way to assess the importance of an issue is to examine crosstabs of each issue and assess whether the issue in question has a significant impact on vote choice. The following example (table 7.8) compares two issues and indicates their impact on the vote. Opinions on abortion divide voters, but the impact is relatively small. Those who are pro-choice are more supportive of the Democrat by 11 percentage points (41.7 percent to 30.8 percent), while those pro-life support a Republican by 14 percentage points (44.7 percent to 30.6 percent). While the issue divides voters, the division is not as great as that for the sports complex issue. The divisions on that issue result in differences of 38 to 34 percentage points in support for the candidates. A candidate may be on the "wrong" side of the abortion issue in this race, but it does not appear that the issue has as much impact as the sports complex issue. If there is an issue the campaign should focus on, at least at this stage of the campaign, it is not the abortion issue. An opponent may seek to make abortion positions an issue, and the impact of the issue needs to be tracked during the campaign, but the issue does not start out having significance to voters.

Finally, a candidate may be on the "wrong" side of the issue (that is, his views are supported by a minority within the district) and the

Table 7.8   The Relative Impact of Issues

| | Candidate Choices | | |
	Democrat	Republican	No Choice
Do you regard yourself as pro-choice or pro-life?			
Pro-choice	41.7	30.8	27.4
Pro-life	30.6	44.7	24.7
No opinion	28.3	35.6	36.1
Local sports stadium–complex: support or oppose?			
Support	18.7	59.4	21.9
Oppose	57.1	25.6	17.3
No opinion	33.5	29.6	36.9

issue has an impact on vote choice. A last resort is for a candidate to try to soften the negative image he receives from his stance on the issue. This might be done by stressing his "positive" positions on other related issues. In the case of abortion, for example, being pro-life can lead to the charge of a man being unconcerned about the situation women face. An opponent may try to portray the man as insensitive to women. The candidate may be supportive of several programs that women favor. The candidate can distribute literature that summarizes his positions on these programs and stress those as often as possible in campaign ads or presentations to try to persuade women that he is sympathetic to their concerns.

Issue Connections

Opinions on one issue may be associated with opinions on another issue. Depending on the situation in the district and the situation of the candidate, a strong connection can be good or bad. Much depends on whether the candidate is on the side of majority opinion. In general, if issues are connected, it may be valuable to tie them together with a more general message to mobilize supporters. If they are unconnected, a general message may not work, but it may be possible to target specific groups with specific messages.

The first matter is how issues are connected. The following (table 7.9) provides an example of two issues that are tied together and two not tied together. The options along the top involve the issue of what should be done to improve schools, an issue faced by many candidates for local offices, the state legislature, and Congress. The question presents voters with the options of more money or higher standards to try to determine a voter's basic inclinations or sympathies. More money involves greater allocations to the schools, while higher standards involves demanding more from teachers or students (which one is not probed for). Along the left are two issues that might be connected. One is whether to respond to a deficit in the local county budget by cutting services or raising taxes. The other is whether county government should continue the existing level of smoking restrictions in public places, or whether more or fewer restrictions should be imposed.

Table 7.9   Connections Among Issues

	Do schools need more money or higher standards?		
Issues and Alternatives	Money	Standards	No Opinion
County has a deficit: cut services or raise taxes?			
Cut services	18.7	59.4	21.9
Raise taxes	62.9	11.3	25.8
No opinion	37.6	25.6	36.8
Should the county retain current or impose fewer or more smoking restrictions?			
Fewer	33.5	41.6	24.9
Current	38.2	37.5	24.3
More	42.7	35.6	21.7
No opinion	38.0	39.1	22.9

Connected Issues

In the first set of relationships above there is a connection between opinions, while in the second there is virtually none. Those who support cutting services also support higher standards for schools (59.4 percent) over more money (18.7 percent). Those who support a tax increase also support more money for schools (62.9 percent) over standards (11.3 percent). The responses to the schools are associated with views about how to solve the county deficit problem. Further, the connection in the first case "makes sense," indicating there may be a logical basis for using the two issues together during the campaign. For the first issue, those who support cutting services as a response to a deficit are probably conservative (that should be checked using the responses to the question of self-identified political philosophy), and they are strongly supportive of tougher standards rather than more money for schools. The standards response tends to be the conservative response, and it should also be checked to see if that association exists. With these two issues, there is a connection, and there is a *potential* for a connected message for either a conservative or a liberal candidate here.

A liberal is more inclined to favor maintaining government services and support for schools. A liberal rarely seeks to advocate a tax increase just to enact one, but faced with situations which prompt a need for a response (a deficit and growing perceptions that schools are not working, regardless of whether it is accurate), will be more inclined to respond with support for a tax increase (Berry and Berry 1990; Stonecash 2002). A liberal might tie these together by using the deficit and concern for schools to make a strong statement about the need to maintain services and improve schools and justify considering a tax increase to achieve those goals. This message could then serve as a basis to mobilize liberals to support him.

A conservative could, of course, see this connection as a basis to mobilize conservatives. She could emphasize the need for discipline—in government and in the schools—and stress the problems high taxes create for individuals and for the attractiveness of communities. That message could serve to define the candidate to conservatives and mobilize them to vote for her. In both cases, the candidate could see a connection and see the basis for a more general message that will tell voters where the candidate stands and bring voters to them as supporters.

Campaigns are rarely this simple, however. The candidates may not be a clear conservative and a clear liberal. One may support more money for schools but be strongly opposed to more taxes and not be able to tie the issues together. Perhaps most important, while the issues may be connected, there is the crucial issue of the "marginals," or the percentage within the district supporting these alternatives. If a majority or a substantial percentage does not support both service cuts and higher standards, this appeal will mobilize conservatives, but it will not be enough to create a majority to win. The candidate may still want to use these issues to mobilize his natural base, but more will be necessary. The same applies to a liberal. A majority may not support the two positions, making it difficult to use these issues to win a campaign.

If some connective theme is possible, the candidate must then have adequate campaign funds for mailings and television, so that a repeated message tying the issues together can be disseminated. It will not suffice to go to smaller-scale personal presentations and make the case, because the thematic presentation will not reach enough people.

Unconnected Issues

Issues may not be connected, much like the relationship between smoking regulations and the schools in table 7.9. As shown in the bottom half of the table, opinions about smoking restrictions have only a modest relationship to how to improve the schools. Those who want fewer smoking restrictions are more supportive of higher standards (41.6 percent higher standards to 33.5 percent more money), while those who want more restrictions are more supportive of additional funds (42.7 percent more money to 35.6 percent higher standards), but the differences are small and not worth focusing on. Candidates faced with this have two choices. One, they may focus just on the issue that is most important to them and try to use it to build an identity and mobilize likely supporters. Or two, it is not at all unusual to select a few issues that appeal to separate constituencies, to emphasize them and use them to build a majority (coalition might be too strong a word) of voters.

Issue–Candidate Connections in a Majority Party District

Once the connections among issues have been assessed, the next concern is the connection to vote choice. For a candidate with positions on several issues, running in a jurisdiction in which her party has the majority of enrollment, the important matters are whether those positions are supported by her party and whether those supporting her positions have made a connection of those positions with her. The answers to each of these questions indicate what her campaign strategy should be.

The first matter is whether her party supports her positions, so that she can mobilize their support by stressing the issues. Assume, for example, the candidate is a female Republican who favors the general Republican position of tax cuts. She is running for the state legislature and wants to make the case for a tax cut to make the state more attractive to business. It might just be presumed that Republicans favor that approach. The role of polling is to check if that is actually the case. The example in table 7.10 indicates the extent of Republican support for a tax cut. Republicans strongly support her position. An appeal to Republican voters is "preaching to the choir." Stressing this issue will not require voters to cross party lines to support her.

Table 7.10   Party Support for Issues

Q. Some argue that we need to cut the state income tax to make the state more attractive as a place to live, while others think it won't make much difference. Do you think a tax cut will help attract people or not make much difference?

	Will Help	*No Difference*	*No Opinion*
Party Registration			
Republican	65.8	17.4	16.8
Independent	51.4	27.3	21.3
Democrat	23.6	48.7	27.7

Q. Do you regard yourself as pro-life or pro-choice?

	Pro-life	Pro-choice	No Opinion
Party Registration			
Republican	61.1	24.8	14.1
Independent	33.5	53.4	13.1
Democrat	25.6	67.1	7.3

The crosstab of party by all issues will indicate the extent of party support for various issue positions. For some issues the differences between Republicans and Democrats will be less. In the example below, the differences by party on each issue are significant. For the tax cut (65.8 percent of Republicans support a tax cut, while only 23.6 percent of Democrats support it), the difference is 42.2 percentage points, and for the abortion issue the difference on pro-life positions is 35.5 percentage points. Most Republicans support tax cuts and the pro-life position, and appealing to them on these issues means appealing to a substantial majority of them and alienating few of them. If they are a majority of the jurisdiction, appealing to them could serve to mobilize them and provide the bulk of a majority. On other issues the division of opinion among Republicans might be 51 percent support for position A versus 33 percent support for position B, for a difference of only 18 percentage points. Party support is not strong and there is considerable opposition. If a substantial percentage of Democrats support position B, an approach might be taken of making an appeal to them, across parties, in the hope that enough Democrats will cross party lines on that issue to make up for those Republicans not mobilized by the issue. Campaigns often decide to do that, but it means assuming partisans from the other party will defect.

This issue compatibility found on the tax matter may not exist on other issues. Assume that this female Republican candidate is also pro-choice. The table indicates Republicans in this jurisdiction are fairly strong in their support of the pro-life position, while Democrats strongly support the pro-choice position. This issue will not serve as a means to mobilize Republican support.

These differences in party support for positions the candidate has taken provide the basis for forming a campaign plan. As noted earlier, candidates do not take polls and then decide whether to maintain or change their positions. They decide which issues to emphasize and to whom. On the tax cut, the issue will connect with Republican voters, and campaign literature should be sent to Republicans to communicate her commitment to that issue. A second issue might not have as strong support among Republicans, and considerable discussion may take place on whether this issue might attract Independents and Democrats and not alienate Republicans. The decision might be to give the issue considerable emphasis to pull crossover votes. If the issue is that of smoking regulations and both the Republican and the Democratic candidates favor more restrictions, then the logic may be that Republican voters "have nowhere to go" for a conservative alternative and stressing support for smoking restrictions may well be a crucial issue to create Democratic party defections and insure a majority. Others within the campaign will argue that stressing this position, as Republican voters are trying to learn who the candidate is, might reduce their enthusiasm and lead many of them to not volunteer, not contribute, and stay home on election day. This might prompt further analysis, using voter registration files, of whether Republicans opposed to more restrictions regularly vote. If they do not, then they are of less concern and the candidate may stress the issue to try to generate crossover votes. If they do vote regularly, then a discussion has to occur over whether an emphasis on this issue will alienate them, or whether they are unlikely to defect because the other candidate does not represent a party they like or a choice they find more attractive.

The abortion issue provides another difficult matter. This is presumably more of an emotional and motivating issue, and a female pro-choice Republican might hope that it will not become an issue. That may work because a Democrat who is pro-choice is unlikely to call attention to her position because noting that they are both pro-choice will pull Republican voters to him. If this happens, the issue may not emerge as significant in the race, and the Republican will hope her party supporters will just live with her position. On the other hand, if the results of this poll or subsequent polls show that the Republican is not doing well with Independent and Democratic women, the campaign may decide, at a later time during the campaign, to send a letter to Independent and Democratic women from a prominent, relatively nonpartisan set of women, summarizing her record and noting her pro-choice position in the letter. This has to be carefully considered and perhaps done late in the campaign because the Democrat may make an issue of it and call her a hypocrite. On the other hand, the campaign may not want to wait too long, because candidate preferences may solidify and the letter may arrive too late to have any impact. These issues usually engender considerable discussion, with the decision often put off to see what polls in late September and early October show.

The analysis up to this point assesses just the compatibility of issues and party support. That analysis suggests possibilities. The next concern is whether connections have developed between issues and vote choice. Do voters connect a candidate with the issue positions expected, or does the campaign face the challenge of making that connection? If a Democratic candidate believes that government services need to be maintained and that a tax increase would therefore be justified (and an opponent favors service cuts and no tax increase), do voters make that connection? Do they see a distinction between the candidates and see the Democrat as the choice to maintain services? The following example (table 7.11) indicates two different situations that can occur for a candidate in the earlier stages of a campaign. Assume that the earlier analysis found strong support among Republicans for service cuts and among Democrats to maintain services.

Situation A is a very common one at the beginning of a campaign. The issue may have just emerged, and the candidates may have just

Table 7.11   Issues and Vote Choice: Responses to How to Respond to County Deficit
(Cut services or raise taxes) and Vote Choice

	Candidate Choices		
	Democrat	Republican	No Choice
Situation A			
Cut services	33.5	41.6	24.9
Raise taxes	41.2	34.5	24.3
No opinion	42.7	35.6	21.7
Situation B			
Cut services	24.9	58.3	16.8
Raise taxes	61.4	17.3	21.3
No opinion	33.6	38.7	27.7

announced their positions on the issue. They may have received only
one day of news coverage, and the electorate may be paying little
attention to the campaign. The combination of limited position presentation and limited newspaper coverage results in voters having no
sense of who supports what alternative, and issue positions have little
connection to vote choice. This is a situation that can lead to different
interpretations. It could be that the issue does not matter very much
to voters and does not affect vote choice. Respondents have an opinion on the issue, but they do not see the issue as very important, and
it does not affect how they are likely to vote. In part it is possible to
assess that by asking about a number of issues and asking which ones
are most important to them. It could also be that the issue is not seen
as important now, but it could become more important as the campaign proceeds through media coverage or one of the campaigns
wishes to make it more important. The Democrat may see the need to
develop a connection, both to mobilize potential voters and to pre-
vent the Republican from dominating the discussion and mobilizing
conservatives. In this case, the campaign of the Democrat has a lot of
work to do to communicate its candidate's position.

In situation B the issue has a significant effect on vote choice. This
may be because there is already a significant ideological party polarization in the area, and that prompts voters with different opinions to
choose candidates by party without really knowing much about them.
Or, it may be because the issue has already been a subject of much
discussion. The campaign should discuss the attention the issue has
received and consider whether the support the Democrat is receiving

is really support for the candidate, or just a reflection of party differences. If it is likely to be the latter, then the campaign still has a lot of work to do to make sure the issue–vote choice connection is strong. It cannot just be presumed that a connection will continue.

In general, the primary task of a candidate in a jurisdiction with a majority of party registration is to find, among those issues the candidate wishes to emphasize, those that are best suited to mobilize his party base. He then needs to make sure that his positions on those issues are communicated to build support among likely supporters. In same cases the connection may already exist, while in others developing the connection will require money.

Candidates cannot, however, assume that they can just focus on the issues that will gain them support and that they have no vulnerabilities. An opponent, if adequately financed, will recognize her status as the underdog and will be looking for his vulnerabilities. If, for example, the Democratic candidate has been in political office before, he will have a record and public positions on a number of issues. The Republican is likely to do research about the opponent's previous public positions and know that record. The Democrat needs to ask questions about his past votes and positions, if he thinks the opponent will focus on those matters. The concern is that voters might react negatively to any of them. If so, the campaign can prepare a plan in case the Republican begins to attack on those issues. In essence the Democrat needs to conduct much the same analysis that his Republican opponent is likely to do to try to anticipate attacks.

Issue–Candidate Connections in a Minority Party District

Most voters registered in a party tend to vote for the candidate of their party. A candidate who begins a race in a jurisdiction in which his party is in the minority faces a difficult challenge. She must either have a weak, little-known opponent and a considerable advantage in name recognition and ratings, or she must find some way to move some partisans away from their normal behavior. If she is not as well known and her party is in the minority, then issues are the means by which voters might be moved.

The first step for a campaign is to find those issues that can move voters away from their normal partisan behavior. This begins with discussions with the campaign staff, starting with those doing the opposition research. They bring the collection of material they have found, and there is a discussion about the accuracy of the information and the likely value of each vote or position as a means of pulling voters. In an ideal world, a poll might ask about many different positions. Again, however, polls cost money, and it is necessary to choose some issues to focus on even before writing the script. There is also a problem with respondent fatigue. A campaign may have lots of money, but there are limits as to how long respondents will stay on the phone, so even with lots of money there are some limits.

The initial poll should then ask questions in which voters are either asked for their position on an issue, or they are informed of the opponent's record and asked if knowing that makes them more or less favorable to (or more or less likely to vote for) the opponent. If the latter approach is taken, then at the end of the poll, the matchup question might be asked again, and the respondent might be asked—if he changed his vote choice—which of several issues made him change his mind.

Each of these approaches provides a means to assess whether an issue might potentially be used to move voters. It is never possible, of course, to be certain that an issue will move voters. An underdog Democrat might be pro-choice and a Republican might be pro-life, and the majority of voters are pro-choice. The Democrat may then be sure that she can attack the Republican over his position because the poll shows that people do not agree with his position, and she can therefore pull pro-choice supporters away from the Republican. The difficulty is that the issue may not be that salient or significant to voters, so that the issue will strongly affect their vote. Voters may say an issue is important to them, but it may not affect their vote choice that much.

With that caution in mind, the two approaches of asking about issues and assessing the vote connection, or specifically presenting an opponent's record and asking about its effect, provide the basis for deciding what issues might be used to create a contrast between the two candidates. Using the first approach, the results might indicate that 57 percent of respondents are pro-choice and 25 percent are pro-life. The crosstab of respondent positions with vote choice may show, as it often does for issues early in a campaign and as shown in table 7.12, that at this juncture there is no association between voter posi-

Table 7.12   Looking for Issues to Move Voters: Abortion and Vote Choice

	Candidate Choices		
	Democrat	*Republican*	*No Choice*
Respondent's Position on Abortion: Current			
Pro-choice (57%)	41.6	33.5	24.9
Pro-life (25%)	34.5	41.2	24.3
No opinion (18%)	42.7	35.6	21.7
Respondent's Position on Abortion: Hoped for Change			
Pro-choice (57%)	68.5	22.4	9.1
Pro-life (25%)	19.6	64.7	15.7
No opinion (18%)	42.7	35.6	21.7

tion on abortion and vote choice. Indeed, it is even possible that with most of the electorate not paying a great deal of attention, or unaware of the candidates, voters who oppose a position of the candidate could still be supporting him out of ignorance. In the first situation shown below, with a majority favoring the pro-choice issue and the opponent pro-life, there is the possibility that the Democrat can run ads indicating that she favors the right of women to choose, while her opponent does not favor that right. The goal is to identify a position with the opponent and use the abortion issue to move supporters of the pro-choice position to the Democrat. If this works successfully, then by the end of the campaign, it should be possible to create an electoral division as shown in the bottom half of the table. Those pro-choice have moved to be strong supporters of the Democrat.

This approach involves making a decision about issues that are likely to matter to voters. It assumes that a campaign can work to define an opponent by identifying what he stands for and then pull voters away from the opponent with that issue. This might be done using votes on various issues such as tax increases, program cuts or increases, building a sports stadium, or approving an appointment. It also involves announced positions or statements the opponent has made.

An alternative is to ask whether specific attributes of the opponent or his record make respondents more likely to vote for the candidate or for his opponent. These responses provide an indication of which issues may move voters more, if information about these matters can be communicated to voters. As discussed earlier, these questions can be asked, and then the matchup can be asked again, to see if information does have the impact expected. The following example (table 7.13) provides a summary of such questions, along with the net impact of information on the vote for a Democratic candidate. The responses indicate that the Democrat has an advantage on the basis of his elective experience but that being in his seventies and from a wealthy family is detrimental. The Republican is not helped by being a lawyer, or working for a big law firm, or having no elective experience. He is helped by being relatively young. The net numbers indicate whether the information favors the Democrat (a plus number) or hurts the Democrat (a negative number). The information indicates what the Democrat will want to stress (his experience) and avoid (his age and images that make that evident, and his family wealth). The information also indicates what message the Democrat may want to use against the Republican (inexperience and ties to a big law firm).

Table 7.13   Reaction to Candidate Traits

Q. Now I'd like to try something different. I'll read you some characteristics of the two candidates in this race, and for each could you tell me if you would be more or less likely to vote for [the Democrat] or [the Republican]. If it won't make any difference, please say so. Would you be more or less likely to vote for [the Democrat] or [the Republican] if . . .

	Democrat	No Difference	Republican	No Opinion	Net
1. the Republican is a lawyer	27.0	51.8	16.5	4.7	10
2. the Republican works for a law firm that represents large corporations, such as utilities and tobacco companies	73.7	20.4	3.9	2.0	70
3. the Democrat comes from a wealthy family	3.7	72.1	20.2	3.9	−17
4. the Democrat is in his seventies	3.7	34.0	60.6	1.7	−57
5. the Republican is in his thirties	5.6	43.0	35.7	1.7	−30
6. the Republican has never run for office before	23.7	58.8	14.1	3.5	10
7. the Democrat has been elected to local office, such as town supervisor and county legislator	65.3	29.1	3.5	2.2	62

Finally, to assess the actual impact of information and not presume an impact, the last analysis should be to assess how much information really moves voters. Assume the Democrat is in a situation where the party registration favors the Republican. The Democrat must find what information he can use to try to move voters away from voting for a Republican. He is also worried that the Republican will run television ads presenting a contrast of the two, using a grainy picture of the Democrat that makes him look old. The concern is whether the age issue really matters to voters. There is reason to think it may not matter that much because most voters are older, and they may not respond to that issue as much as they say. Table 7.14 presents the first and second matchup responses by the responses to the age and experience questions. The first matchup shows some relationship between the responses and the initial matchup, which is probably because those saying they are more likely to vote for a Democrat were already favorable to a Democratic candidate. Those saying they are more favorable to a Republican were already more favorable to a Republican.

The crucial matter is how voters with different responses to questions respond to the second matchup. If information affects voters, then it should be that those with specific responses make very different vote choices in the second matchup. If the age of the Democrat matters to those who say it matters, they should be much less supportive of him in the second matchup. Those more likely to vote for the Democrat because of his age should be more positive. With regard to experience, those who say the Democrat's experience matters should shift

Table 7.14   Comparing First and Second Matchups

	First Matchup		Second Matchup	
	Republican	Democrat	Republican	Democrat
Overall	32.8	24.4	38.9	39.7
Age of Democrat				
More likely Democrat	45.3	16.6	51.1	22.4
No difference	18.5	22.2	20.8	37.7
More likely Republican	13.7	44.1	24.6	49.1
Experience of Democrat				
More likely Democrat	21.9	25.6	22.4	55.1
No difference	22.0	24.1	35.6	37.5
More likely Republican	38.9	23.3	44.7	24.6

to him, while those who say it doesn't matter should
nificantly.

The results in the table suggest that age does not matter
as people say, but that experience does matter. The table compares the
vote choices of voters for the first and second matchup questions in
the poll. The comparisons are by reactions to how much age and experience matter. Those who say the age of the Democrat makes them
less likely to vote for the Democrat provide change from 13.7 percent
Republican and 44.1 percent Democrat on the first matchup, to 24.6
percent Republican and 49.1 percent Democrat on the second matchup. While the Republican gains 10.9 percentage points, the Democrat also gains, increasing 5 percentage points. Knowing about age
does not shift the vote choice. Experience, however, appears to have a
greater impact. Among those saying that his experience makes them
more likely to vote for the Democrat, the matchup changes from 21.9
percent Republican and 25.6 percent Democrat, to 22.4 percent
Republican and 55.1 percent Democrat. The Republican gains less
than 1 percentage point while the Democrat gains almost 30 points.
The results suggest that, at least for now, the Democrat does not have
to worry about his age. He should continually stress his experience
and his ability to use that experience to represent the area. He should
also make it clear that his opponent has no experience.

Finally, the results can be checked even further to see who
changed. Are those who changed their vote choices to the Democrat
(from either undecided or the other candidate) Democrats, Independents, or Republicans? If they are all Democrats, it means that this
information helps them decide to vote for the candidate of their party.
If this is the case, the issue will help shore up his base, but it will not do
much to attract Independents and Republicans. If the changed votes
include a substantial percentage of Independents and Republicans,
then the information provides the content of a message to attract these
two groups of voters. This same approach to analysis can be used to
assess an opponent's votes cast, positions taken, or policy proposals
made.

These two approaches (asking about issues and assessing the vote
connection) provide alternative ways of trying to determine if there
are issues that a candidate or a party can use to pull voters away from
another candidate or party. The first does not specifically ask about
impact or ask about a second matchup, while the second does. It may

seem that the second would be the preferred approach, because there is more apparent certainty about results. Despite that appearance, it is an approach that has its limits. Conducting surveys with lots of positive and negative information about candidates can be a valuable guide to what information affects people, but it also is artificial. Some respondents do not like the approach and object during the process if they see a statement of "fact" as biased. This approach usually occurs early in a campaign before voters have devoted much attention to an issue. The process has its limits because it presents voters with information that they may not receive during a campaign because they do not pay attention or their partisan attachment leads them to diminish the value of the information. The process also does not capture the role of the opponent in presenting a counter message during a campaign. In short, the exercise may be too artificial to produce reliable results. Even if it is valid, the candidate may not have the money during the campaign to present all this information. For all these reasons, the results may not be as valid as a candidate hopes. They suggest the impact of information, but the results should be accepted with some caution.

Many times candidates or parties use the first approach and simply decide that focusing on an issue, regardless of what current polls show, will be valuable. The issue may be valuable for the candidate or party because it will mobilize their base by reinforcing loyalties and the opponent or opposition party will be seen as vulnerable on the issue. The poll results may show a possible opening for the party, but they also show that the candidate or party will have to work to make the issue prominent, connect the opponent to the issue, and use it to move voters.

The situation of Senate Democrats in the summer of 2002 provides an example. Following the terrorist attacks of September 11, 2001, George Bush's ratings soared. While they were gradually declining in subsequent months, they were still very high (approximately 70 percent approved of his job performance in July), and Democrats were struggling to come up with some issues to use to criticize Republicans. Finding some issues was very important because Democrats held the Senate by a small margin and were close to a majority in the House. In the summer of 2002, corporate scandals became an issue of considerable concern. Corporate officers were accused of inflating revenues to make profits look better, and as word of this spread, the stock market steadily declined. Polls during early July provided mixed evidence about how much this would hurt Republicans. When asked if "big business had too much influence on _____," the responses for the Bush administration were 63 percent yes to 32 percent no, for Democrats in Congress they were 64 percent yes to 28 percent no, and for Republicans in Congress they were 76 percent yes to 16 percent no. The public thought big business had too much influence on all three, with Democrats having no great claim to being less influenced.[2] That same poll showed high confidence that President Bush would take effective action to make corporations responsible. But that same poll also found that when respondents were asked if Democrats in Congress / Republicans in Congress were more interested in protecting ordinary Americans or large corporations, the responses were, for Democrats, 55 percent ordinary Americans—36 percent large corporations, and for Republicans they were 30 percent ordinary Americans—62 percent large corporations. Polls later in the month found more concern about the economy, some slide in Bush's ratings, concern that business had too much influence on Bush, and a continuing sense that Republicans were more concerned with protecting large corporations.[3]

In this case polls provided information that this issue might have the potential to serve as a means to pry voters away from Republicans, making it an attractive line of attack for Democrats. It is not just an opportunistic, poll-driven attack, however. The Democratic constituency tends to be less affluent and probably more likely to see corporations in a negative way (party polling would tell that). Attacking corporations and Republican favoritism to them could serve to reinforce existing beliefs and loyalties among Democrats. If so, it could mobilize them to vote in November and perhaps provide a sufficient margin in enough districts to win control of the House of Representatives. Thus, even if current poll results do not demonstrate that the issue is affecting voters, pursuing the issue can serve the needs of the party (solidifying support) and allow it to define its interests more clearly to the electorate. Republicans, of course, read the same polls and were quick to agree to legislation in August 2002, imposing more rules and regulations on corporations. Whether the issue of corporate scandals would continue to be relevant would be told only by subsequent tracking polls, but at least at that juncture in the campaign, the issue had considerable potential for Democrats, and they chose to push the issue in campaigns.

Notes

1. Results taken from the Quinnipiac Poll accessed at www.quinnipiac.edu/polls/trend/nytrend.html.

2. David Moore, "Little Political Fallout from Business Scandals," Gallup Poll Analysis, July 8, 2002. www.gallup.com/poll/releases/pr020708.asp?Version=p

3. Richard W. Stevenson and Janet Elder, "Poll Finds Concerns That Bush Is Overly Influenced by Business," *New York Times*, July 18, 2002, A1; David Moore, "Business Scandals Appear to Hurt Republicans in Congressional Race," Gallup Poll Analysis, July 30, 2002. www.gallup.com/poll/releases/pr020730.asp?Version=p

Reports and Recommendations   8

⭐🏴

T HE PURPOSE OF INITIAL POLLS is to gather information that will provide the basis for a campaign plan. The report that is presented to a campaign manager and the candidate should boil all the information down to that purpose. Reports should be relatively short—ten to twenty pages—with only the essential information included. Campaign managers generally want you to interpret the results and provide them with an overview and suggestions. They do not want to walk through all the results. They do not want a long and tedious analysis.

Reports should tell the candidate where she stands now and what specific actions need to be taken to win. The candidate needs to know her name recognition and ratings and how she compares with the opponent. She needs to know the matchup and who supports her and who does not. She needs to know who she needs to bring to her side and what issues she might use to do that. Finally, the report should include a summary of the calling process and the sample derived and a copy of the survey, so there will be no ambiguity about the questions asked and the order of the questions. The usual sections of a report are shown below. A complete report is in the appendix.

REPORT CONTENTS
- Name recognition, candidate ratings, the matchup, and relevant crosstab results for these responses.
- The issues, organized conceptually. It is not a good idea to simply walk through each question. If questions involve a similar issue, report them together, comment on their connections (from the crosstabs), and explain the political significance and possibilities for the candidate and the campaign strategy.
- Recommendations of what the campaign must do to change the results, or keep doing to maintain a situation.
- A summary of how the sample compares to the population initially sampled.
- A copy of the survey.

Aside from that general format, each campaign is unique. In each case, the situations of party registration, the comparison of initial candidate name recognition, ratings, the matchup results, and the dominant issues within the jurisdiction dictate the approach that must be taken to the analysis and the report. The crucial matter is to present the results as a narrative that takes the campaign from where it is now to how it can get to where it wants to be.

The following are examples of different situations that candidates face and different matters they must focus on during the campaign. The first example involves a very typical situation of a candidate not as well known as the opponent. The candidate must focus primarily on building her name recognition and developing greater support among her base. The second example involves a challenger losing to an incumbent. He needs to find some issues that will allow him to erode the incumbent's lead. The third example involves a candidate who is running for mayor and finds that, while he is doing well, the specific policy options he wishes to pursue deal with a serious budget problem that will alienate his core supporters. His challenge is to disseminate his message of fiscal restraint but avoid discussing specifics that could drive away an electorate not yet convinced it is necessary to raise fees and taxes.

Report Example 1: A Problem of Name Identification and Mobilizing a Base

In this example, two fairly well-known candidates are involved. The Republican begins the race with lower name recognition and not doing as well among her own party as the Democrat is doing among his party registrants. The district is equally divided in party registration among likely voters. The report focuses on her primary task, which is improving name recognition and support among Republicans.

Name Recognition, Ratings, and the Matchup

The Democrat begins this race with an advantage over the Republican (table 8.1). His name recognition is 90 percent (10 percent have never heard of him), while hers (the Republican) is 84 percent (16 percent

have not heard of her). About 24 percent have no opinion of him, while 31 percent have no opinion of her. The result is that 66 percent have some opinion of the Democrat, while only 53 percent have some opinion of the Republican. His ratings are also very good, at 57 percent favorable to 9 percent unfavorable, while hers are only 39 percent to 14 percent. While she begins with a disadvantage, it is not a significant disadvantage. About 47 percent have never heard of her or have no opinion, while his combined percentage is 34. If she can covert a reasonable percentage of the 47 percent into favorable evaluations, she will be in a situation very similar to his. Given the amount of time remaining before the campaign heats up (sometime in September), there is plenty of opportunity to generate name recognition and ratings similar to his.

The Republican has a significant advantage in visibility in town D, but she has a long way to go to match him in towns A, B, and C. The next several months have to be devoted to increasing her name recognition in towns B and C, because these are areas where she has a good chance of winning votes, if she is better known.

Table 8.1   Candidate Name Recognition and Ratings

	Favorable	Unfavorable	No Opinion	Never Heard Of
Republican	38.9	13.6	30.8	16.8
Democrat	57.0	9.4	23.5	10.1
Area: Republican				
Town A	24.2	14.1	40.4	21.2
Town B	38.9	20.8	23.6	16.7
Town C	35.9	8.5	34.0	21.7
Town D	52.7	13.2	24.8	9.3
Area: Democrat				
Town A	69.7	11.1	13.1	6.1
Town B	71.8	8.5	16.9	2.8
Town C	63.2	16.0	17.0	3.8
Town D	34.1	3.1	40.3	22.5

The Democrat's advantage in name recognition is not just geographical (see table 8.2). He does much better among some groups, which is to be expected, but he also does better in unexpected ways. He has higher name recognition and better ratings among Democrats, liberals, and women, all of which are to be expected. He does better even among those younger and those who do not vote in every elec-

Table 8.2   Vote Choice by Groups

Q 5. This November [ ], the Democrat, will run against [ ], the Republican, for the [#] Assembly seat. Would you most likely vote for [the Democrat] or [the Republican]?

	Democrat	*Republican*	*No Opinion*
Overall	46.3	26.5	27.2
Party			
Republican	27.7	46.6	25.7
Independent	46.5	25.6	27.9
Democratic	62.9	8.6	28.5
Area			
Town A	54.6	17.5	27.8
Town B	56.9	19.4	23.6
Town C	52.8	27.4	19.8
Town D	28.7	36.4	34.9
Self-defined Ideology			
Liberal	66.7	10.7	22.7
Moderate	51.7	25.0	23.3
Conservative	30.4	40.2	29.5

tion. The troubling signs for the Republican involve Republicans and self-defined conservatives. These are groups that she has to win, and he is now doing better among them than she is. Conservatives are particularly important. Approximately 28 percent of respondents identify themselves as conservatives, while only 19 percent identify themselves as liberals. About 53 percent of conservatives are enrolled as Republicans, and 40 percent of conservatives will vote Republican. As of now, the Democrat does better among Democrats and liberals than the Republican is doing among her base—Republicans and conservatives. That pattern has to be reversed or she will not win this election. Given that 55 percent of likely voters are male, it is also crucial to reduce his advantage among them.

Given the slight Democratic enrollment advantage and his name recognition advantage, the matchup at this point is not as bad as might be expected. He has been in office longer, her prior electoral base has been relatively small, and she has not been in office long. The result is that the Democrat now wins 46 percent to 27 percent. The good news for the Republican is that the Democrat does not get over 50 percent at this time. It will eventually be necessary for her to define him with critical ads, but for now her primary challenge is to increase her name recognition. As with name recognition, he does better among Democrats, liberals, men, and those living in towns A, B, and C. Her problem is that she does not offset that by doing equally as well among Republicans, conservatives, women, and those living in town D. She has to become more visible.

Report Example 2: Finding an Issue to Use against a Frontrunner

In this example, a Republican is running in a city with a Democratic registration advantage. The Republican is behind the Democratic incumbent in the May and August matchups. The Democrat is wisely ignoring the Republican except for a few debates. The Republican has to find an issue to get the electorate to take a serious look at the incumbent. This is an excerpt from the report that deals with the only issue that has the potential to get some attention.

The Education Issue

The schools represent a potentially crucial issue. In the open-ended issue question, schools show up overwhelmingly as the most important issue. The newspapers are reporting that the schools now have a $10 million deficit (out of a $200 million budget), and the Democrat has refused to promise he will cover the deficit with city funds. State revenues are falling due to the recession, and there may not be enough state aid to make up for the school shortfall. This provides an excellent opportunity for the Republican to confront the Democrat to ask tough questions about leadership and how finances are going to be handled in a time of stress. It would also allow the Republican to shift the focus to a specific policy problem and question the Democrat's commitment to schools. A contrast about the willingness to support schools could be particularly valuable in pulling Democrats away from the incumbent. Democrats are much more worried about education (64 percent compared to 45 percent for Republicans), and a contrast could get some of them to defect.

The emphasis cannot be just on more money, however. When we

ask people what they want to do about schools, more support tougher standards than support more spending (table 8.3). The Republican has come out in favor of higher standards, so he could couple his willingness to provide the necessary support for schools with a strong commitment to require more from schools in exchange.

Table 8.3   Education Policy Alternatives

Q 15. The mayoral candidates are talking about the need to improve the city public schools. If you were mayor, would your first priority be spending more money to hire teachers and rebuild schools, or would it be to set higher standards for students and teachers?

Spend more	36.8
Higher standards	41.8
Both	15.1
No opinion	6.2

This is also an issue that could be used to mobilize Republicans and Independents. Democrats support more spending over standards 46 percent to 34 percent, while Republicans are 28 percent more spending to 51 percent higher standards, and Independents are 29 percent to 42 percent. Divisions on this issue also coincide with the Republican's natural electoral base. The Northside, which is more Republican, is 30 percent more spending to 49 percent higher standards. In the West Side it is 37 percent spending to 44 percent standards, and in the South Side it is 35 percent to 40 percent. These areas have divided party registration. The East Side, heavily Democratic, is 49 percent spending to 31 percent standards. A focus on supporting schools but asking for more could mobilize Republicans, and draw enough Democrats to make this a race.

Report Example 3: Selective Emphasis of Issues

In this example, a Republican was running in a city facing a serious budget problem. For many years the city derived most of its budget revenue from a public utility, which was willing to pay taxes, because it just passed the expense on to consumers. The utility had been purchased by another firm, which had successfully challenged the high tax rate, and the city was facing a major loss of revenues. The drop had not yet occurred, so, despite many newspaper stories of impending crisis, residents had experienced no changes in their situations. The Republican candidate firmly believed that residents had to face the end of many free services such as water. The problem the poll revealed was that most residents perceived that the city budget problems were largely a product of waste. There was strong opposition to requiring water meters, and the Republican's support came primarily from those who opposed metered water. As often happens, the candidate found an electorate perceiving a budget problem, but not convinced that one of his proposals, metered water, was necessary. The candidate had to do what many candidates must do: emphasize a general theme of making tough decisions and cutting the budget, but hold off on the proposal to impose fees for services until he had enough time to engage in a sustained effort to convince voters that something more serious was necessary.

While some see this as deception and a lack of courage on the part of the candidate, it involves caution and respect in dealing with the public. Most voters do not follow public policy debates closely, and newspapers do not consistently cover them. Persuading the public that a serious problem exists takes time. Many political figures realize this and know they must carefully communicate the severity of a problem through repeated stories. When leaders pledge to be decisive or act that way in office, without developing this acceptance, they often lose elections (Stonecash 2002).

The Budget Situation

While the impending loss of public utility revenue clearly presents a serious problem, not everyone sees it as serious (table 8.4). About 55 percent see it as requiring major fee and tax increases, but 38 percent think the problem can be solved with modest increases. Republicans are more impressed with the seriousness of the situation (45 percent modest changes to 54 percent major) than Democrats (52 percent modest to 39 percent major). Lower-income voters are less convinced this is a serious problem than are high-income voters. These divisions create the potential for a Democrat to conduct a campaign arguing that modest changes will solve the budget problem. A Democrat will find Democrats and city workers and their families receptive to that message.

Table 8.4   The Budget Crisis and General Approaches

Q 4. As you probably know, the city of [ ] will lose much of its tax revenue from the [ ] steam station. I'd like to ask you how serious you think this lost revenue is for the city budget. Some argue the city budget can be roughly maintained as is and lost revenues can replaced with modest tax and fee increases each year. Others argue it will take immediate and major increases in fees and taxes to maintain the current budget. Do you think maintaining the budget will require modest or major fee and tax increases?

Modest	38.3
Major	55.5
No opinion	6.2

Q 5. Is the best way to solve future budget problems to focus on cutting the city budget, or should the focus be on increases in fees and taxes to replace lost revenue. *(Do not offer "both" or "combination," but record.)*

Cutting the budget	50.5
Both / combination	15.5
Fees and taxes	20.2
No opinion	13.8

Q 6. Do you think the city budget has so much waste that cuts can be made without hurting services, or do you think there isn't that much waste and cuts will significantly reduce services?

Budget has waste	47.5
Significant reductions	37.8
No opinion	14.7

The problem for the Republican is that as of now the electorate does not support his proposals for how to solve the budget problem. While he wants to impose water meter and sewer fees, the consensus is that the primary approach should be budget cuts and that there is enough waste in the budget to make cuts without serious reductions in services. Party and ideology also play a role in these reactions. Republicans are more likely to support cuts (70 percent cuts, 8 percent combination of cuts and fee and tax increases) than are Democrats (41 percent cuts to 26 percent fees and taxes). Liberals support fee and tax increases (32 percent) more than conservatives (4 percent). The same pattern prevails for the existence of waste, with Republicans and conservatives more inclined to see waste and Democrats and liberals less inclined.

The problem for the Republican is that his likely electoral base is the most likely to agree with him that there is a serious problem, but least likely to support the solutions he is proposing.

Fee and Tax Increases

When asked about specific solutions, there is little support for establishing fees or for increasing property taxes (table 8.5). The proposal with the highest support is that for establishing water fees, with only 35 percent support. The levels of support for taxes or fees is even less among likely voters. Among likely voters only 28 percent support water fees, 22 percent support sewer fees, and 12 percent support property tax increases. The greatest support for these increases comes from those who are younger, are Independents, are positive about the direction of the city's economy, and are somewhat more affluent. These groups are also less likely to be regular voters. Democrats and Republicans do not differ much in their response to these proposals, but the Republican's natural constituency is most opposed to these fee and tax increases.

Table 8.5   Fee and Tax Increases

Q. Would you support or oppose the following?

	Support	Oppose	No Opinion
Installing residential water meters, with usage fees, to raise additional revenue?	35.8	52.8	11.4
Establishing sewer fees to raise additional revenue?	30.4	59.2	10.4
Raising local property taxes?	17.1	74.2	8.7

Issues and Election Choices

The problem that the Republican faces is shown in table 8.6. In the matchup, those who are most supportive of budget cuts are most supportive of him, and those who think there is enough waste to resolve the problem are more supportive. Those who oppose property tax increases are more supportive. The Republican holds an advantage among those who want the fiscally conservative position but don't support his proposals. For *most* issues there are more voters who endorse the fiscally conservative position than endorse the liberal position. That is even more the case among likely voters. Much as at the national level, Republicans are seen as the party to take a conservative fiscal approach. He has to exploit that image but hold off on proposing fee and tax increases for now.

Table 8.6   Mayoral Choices by Issue Positions

	Republican	Democrat	Percent with Opinion
Solution to budget problems			
Cuts	39.3	21.3	51.0
Fees and taxes	31.8	27.3	15.0
Waste in budget			
Enough waste	35.2	15.5	48.0
Not so much waste	31.8	27.3	37.5
Support for property tax increases			
Support	17.7	41.2	17.2
Oppose	35.2	24.2	74.0

Tracking Polls and the Undecided   9

B ENCHMARK POLLS PROVIDE the information for creating a
campaign plan. Tracking polls are the means by which a campaign assesses whether the campaign plan is working or needs
to be changed. An initial poll will indicate the visibility of the candidate and who supports her and who does not. It will indicate that
some issues have potential and should be included in future polls and
others should be dropped. The campaign may have thought there was
concern about leadership, the fiscal management of the city or county,
or particular votes taken by a state legislator or member of Congress,
but the poll results indicate little concern about these issues. Generally
if the electorate is not worried about an issue, it will be dropped from
future polls. Sometimes candidates will stick with an issue, with the
belief that they can make it more prominent and significant during
the campaign. Crime, the state of the schools, or lack of economic
development may be seen as serious issues, ones the candidate cares
about and ones seen as having the potential to allow her to speak out,
while also moving the necessary voters.

These initial decisions make it possible to reduce the size of subsequent scripts to focus on the primary concern of the campaign: are
name recognition and ratings rising and particularly among those the
campaign wants to attract, are specific issues remaining important, and
is the campaign making the desired connection on issues to mobilize
the voters needed? Eliminating some questions provides space to track
reactions to the opponent's ads and charges and see if they are having
an effect. Tracking polls are generally shorter than benchmark polls.
Again, polls cost money, but the campaign would like to do as many
polls as possible. If fewer questions are asked, it is possible to conduct
more polls.

Tracking Polls
The essential concern in tracking polls is not the "horserace" or who
is winning, but whether the campaign is developing in the expected

direction so that the candidate is likely to win. The concern is whether the candidate is differentiating himself from the opponent in a way that will bring the expected voters. As noted earlier, tracking polls are portraits of the electorate at a specific time. They are not predictions of where it will end up. Two matters make prediction very difficult. First, there are likely to be, particularly in a close election, events, television ads, mailings, and media coverage that will affect voters and change their preferences. Polls done prior to these events and actions cannot capture the effect of activities that have not yet happened. The concern of tracking polls is to provide information about what the campaign has to do to try to affect voters. The election results are the indication of the effects of campaign activities. Second, any poll will show some percentage that is undecided. It is difficult to anticipate if these voters will actually vote and how they will break.

Tracking information should be organized by date to help the candidate and campaign see how things are progressing. It is important to include as much time perspective information as possible (results from all past polls) so the candidate has some perspective on changes. Candidates are prone to embrace small shifts in their favor and make far too much of small shifts away from them. Sampling produces variation and changes may just be random fluctuations. National polling reports often devote extensive attention to small shifts, seeing them as a trend, when the results could just be normal random variations. Presenting candidates with information organized by date will let them see trends and various fluctuations for themselves. If several polls are done, presenting all results will also get them away from focusing on a change from just the prior poll, rather than whether things are generally moving in the right or wrong direction. The best way to temper reactions is to set up reports so that a trend perspective is included. A simple table with dates along the left and results running down in columns will help the campaign see the broad changes occurring and get them away from focusing on smaller changes since the last poll.

The following example (table 9.1) is from a race of a Democratic incumbent mayor running against a Republican challenger. The Democrat had made several unpopular decisions, and there was considerable worry about the negative effects of the decisions. The polls tracking the matchup with an opponent (who was known a year in advance) showed a significant drop for the incumbent from July of the prior year, with his vote percentage dropping from May through August of the election year. The value of showing the results over time was that it was clear that the challenger was not able to convert doubters about him into support for her. The tracking polls indicated that she had reached a plateau in the middle to high twenties and she was having a hard time getting above that level. The high percentage of undecided was a serious source of concern, but there was no sense that the challenger was improving, so the campaign plan was continued.

Table 9.1   Tracking a Matchup

Combined	7/98	5/99	7/99	8/99	9/99 I	9/99 II	10/99 I	10/99 II
Democrat	54.8	41.4	39.7	36.9	41.9	46.4	45.3	42.8
Republican	26.5	28.9	29.7	25.9	24.9	24.5	24.7	20.1
No initial choice	18.7	29.6	30.7	37.2	33.2	29.1	30.0	37.2

Name Recognition and Ratings

There are several essential matters to follow in tracking polls. The first is name recognition and ratings. Some long-serving incumbents begin with high name recognition and fairly set ratings, but for most candidates there is, or should be, a significant progression during the campaign. Their ratings should increase, and it is crucial that they avoid experiencing a steady rise in their negatives. Candidates also want to track the same matters for their opponents. If the opponent struggles to increase his name recognition and ratings, then it may be possible to run a largely positive campaign and ignore the opponent. If the opponent is experiencing steadily rising name recognition and his ratings are positive, it may be necessary to "go negative" and try to alter the electorate's impression of the opponent.

Defining an Opponent

The following graphs (figure 9.1) provide an example of the effects of an aggressive effort to shape an opponent's image. The opponent began with low visibility. The incumbent campaign knew that the national parties had targeted the race and that the AFL-CIO was rumored to plan to spend close to a million dollars on ads in the district attacking the incumbent. The campaign chose not to wait to see

Figure 9.1 / Example: Trends in Incumbent and Challenger Ratings during the Campaign

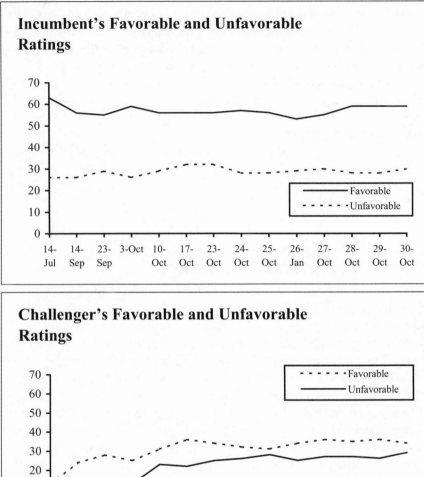

how the opponent's image developed, but to actively define him as the campaign developed. Extensive research was done on his record as a mayor of a town in the district. Several of his decisions were tested early in the campaign, and those found to be seen negatively by the electorate were used in television ads defining him for the electorate. Through tracking polls the campaign was able to track how his ratings changed over time. The expectation was that his name recognition would rise. The goal was to raise his "unfavorables" as the campaign proceeded. The results indicate that the proactive approach worked. The opponent's favorables never became very high during the campaign and his negatives rose steadily, and by November his unfavorable ratings were almost as high as his favorables. He was able to win a substantial proportion of the vote, but he peaked in the low forties and could not climb any higher. The tracking polls allowed the campaign to be sure that the contrast and defining ads were working.

Tracking polls can also be used to try to determine the impact of messages from both campaigns, those of the candidate and the opponent. As noted before, most campaigns are not like the highly visible presidential, Senate, or gubernatorial races. Television is not always the medium for presenting messages. For many campaigns direct mail and literature drops are the primary means of disseminating a message. Since it is not always possible to track the opponent's message by watching television, it is necessary to get friends of the candidate to provide copies of the direct mail that an opposing campaign is distributing. This lets the campaign know what claims and attacks are occurring. The crucial question is the impact of the literature on voters. Do they recall it, and does it affect their rating of each candidate and their vote choice? The information is then useful to decide whose literature is working best and to decide if the campaign needs to match the opponent's literature. The following example (table 9.2) involved a race where candidate A was sending a different oversized postcard each week with a new message. Candidate B had decided to send an extensive brochure type of publication outlining all his positions to communicate the seriousness of his policy concerns and the depth of his proposals. The two types were producing different results, with A's literature remembered by a higher percentage of voters. Candidate B adapted by matching candidate A with weekly postcards.

Tracking the Effects of Campaign Literature

Many campaigns do not involve television ads. For many state legislature and congressional races, the district goes across several counties or is just part of a large metropolitan area. Television does not reach many voters in the first situation and reaches far too many irrelevant voters at far too great a cost in the latter situation. This leads to direct mail, oversized postcards, doorhangers, and palm cards. It is valuable to try to track how visible campaign literature is to see if it is having any impact.

Table 9.2 presents results from a poll conducted in late August. Only persistent voters (those who voted in six of the last six general elections) are shown. The poll was conducted for a primary election, so only persistent voters were likely to vote.

At this point in the campaign, it appears that A's literature is having a greater effect. A greater percentage of respondents recall having received his literature. While B's literature, when recalled, is making a better impression, more remember receiving A's literature (42 percent) than remember receiving B's (29 percent). Candidate A appears to be targeting it well. About 65 percent of those voting in six of the last six elections recall his literature. Within town A, 58 percent remember it, and within town D it is 39 percent. The impact of B's literature is not as pronounced. Among those voting in six of six elections, 43 percent remember his literature. Within town B 32 percent recall it and in town D it is 34 percent. Candidate B's campaign should get copies of what A is sending and try to determine if it is the presentation, is he sending with more frequency, or is he sending many small, inexpensive pieces. This is a race of visibility at this point, and it is important to determine what he is doing to get this higher visibility.

Table 9.2   Recall of Receiving Campaign Literature

Q 19. Do you recall receiving any campaign literature from A?
Yes	41.5
No	49.2
Not sure	9.4

Q 21. Do you recall receiving any campaign literature from B?
Yes	28.8
No	60.7
Not sure	11.7

The recall of campaign literature appears to be having an impact. Those who recall A's literature are 40 percent favorable to 3 percent unfavorable to him, and only 26 percent say they have never heard of him. Those who do not recall his literature are 18 percent favorable to 3 percent unfavorable, with 61 percent saying they have never heard of him. For B, those who recall the literature are 35 percent favorable to 3 percent unfavorable, with 26 percent having never heard of him. Those not recalling it are 10 percent favorable to 1 percent unfavorable, and 69 percent never heard of. It appears that whatever A is sending is having a greater impact. Recall of literature also affects the matchup. Among those recalling the Democrat A's literature, the matchup is 33.9 percent Democratic to 13.7 percent Republican, while among those recalling the Republican's literature, it is 32.6 Republican to 22.1 percent Democratic. Those who recall both are 30.5 percent Democrat to 20.3 percent Republican. A's literature is having an impact. It is crucial to find out what he is distributing, how frequently it is going out, and find a way to match it.

Tracking the Matchup

The other crucial matter is the matchup. The overall numbers are, of course, important. The campaign wants to get above 50 percent and stay there. But, as noted earlier, the other important matter is whether the groups that the campaign is trying to attract to the candidate are moving that way. Is a Democrat attracting liberals, women, those in unions, and those who support more spending on schools? If those relationships are not developing, either the candidate's message is not getting out enough, or it is not effective in connecting with voters, or the message of the opponent is neutralizing the message of the candidate. The following (table 9.3) indicates two examples of what could happen. In this district liberals are 40 percent of the district, moderates 35 percent, and conservatives only 25 percent. Liberals and moderates provide an adequate base for winning the election. The goal is to bring them to the candidate, which would be done with literature and ads presenting his liberal positions on a number of issues and contrasting him with the opponent.

In May the Democrat is not doing particularly well drawing liberals or moderates. The electorate does not see much of a difference between the candidates. By July the Democrat is getting 51.5 percent of liberals' votes and 43.7 percent of moderates' votes. He is also losing the votes of conservatives as he differentiates himself from the

Table 9.3 Self-Defined Ideology and Vote Choice

	Democrat	Republican	No Opinion
May			
Liberal	41.5	35.8	22.7
Moderate	36.5	37.3	26.2
Conservative	31.4	39.8	28.8
July			
Liberal	51.5	31.7	16.8
Moderate	43.7	35.4	20.9
Conservative	28.4	45.9	25.7
September			
Liberal	59.7	25.8	14.5
Moderate	48.1	33.6	18.3
Conservative	25.5	54.2	20.3

Republican. By September his percentage among liberals increases to 59.7 and among moderates to 48.1. The campaign plan is working, in that he is attracting the two groups that he wants and losing the group he expects to lose. There is still considerable work to do, however. The message is getting through with the desired effect, but it needs to be repeated over the last two months to make sure the numbers continue to move in the expected direction.

Results might, of course, evolve differently. The opponent might find several votes by the Democrat for tax increases and repeatedly run ads labeling him as a liberal "who never met a tax he didn't like." That could affect moderates who might be uneasy about increased taxes, holding down the Democrat's percentage among moderates. The awareness of ads, plus the pattern of moderates not moving as expected, would probably prompt the campaign to craft a message either explaining the votes or presenting negative information about the opponent to offset the ads about votes for taxes. Very often campaigns, when presented with ads that do capture actual votes taken, decide that "explaining" them may not reduce the damage done, so the best approach is to go negative and make the opponent less attractive.

A candidate can also find his core base appear to erode. The following example (table 9.4) involves a Democratic mayor who came into office in a city near bankruptcy, following Republican rule. She imposed a large tax increase, which polls showed alienated the less affluent and those who said they had not done better over the last several years. It appeared that the affluent thought she had done the right things and were positive about her. Four years later the fiscal crisis had abated, and the city seemed to be improving. In his campaign, the Republican opponent chose to make the need for a tax cut central to his campaign. The poll taken in May indicated that the Democratic incumbent was continuing to receive her strongest support from the more affluent. The poll indicated that the affluent were more likely to be better off and to think that she had done the right thing in raising taxes. The results indicated that those most able to afford a tax increase were the most tolerant of it, but they were also more prone to be Republican. Her efforts had attracted a constituency that was not naturally Democratic. The Republican was probably getting the

Table 9.4   Changes in Vote Choice: May–October, by Income

	Democrat	Republican	No Choice
May			
Less than $20,000	34	24	41
$20 − < $40,000	38	33	29
$40 − < $60,000	52	23	25
$60,000 +	60	20	20
August			
Less than $20,000	40	27	33
$20 − < $40,000	39	31	30
$40 − < $60,000	37	28	35
$60,000 +	36	31	33
September 15–17			
Less than $20,000	52	28	21
$20 − < $40,000	43	27	31
$40 − < $60,000	39	25	36
$60,000 +	48	24	28
October 15			
Less than $20,000	39	34	26
$20 − < $40,000	50	21	29
$40 − < $60,000	47	32	21
$60,000 +	56	16	27
October 25			
Less than $20,000	44	17	39
$20 − < $40,000	41	21	38
$40 − < $60,000	45	30	25
$60,000 +	47	21	32

same results and thought he could attract this constituency. He never let up in his focus on the need for a tax cut.

Subsequent polls indicated that the incumbent's job approval and vote percentage were steadily slipping, with the greatest loss coming among those with higher incomes. The incumbent chose in mid-September to step up criticisms of her Republican challenger as irresponsible and claimed that a tax cut would risk the stability the city had finally achieved. She did not regain her strong support among the affluent, but the erosion of her support among the affluent stopped, and she won a close election.

This example illustrates the importance to being open to all possibilities in reviewing tracking poll results. It would not normally be expected that a Democrat would do better among the affluent, but the results indicated that was the pattern. Electoral bases should be assessed and not presumed. The analysis must also compare current and past crosstabs and search for what issues appear to be having the greatest effect. That is, which issues move voters the most? Are these the issues the campaign expected to be important, and are they likely to continue to be important?

Tracking Polls and Spending

These tracking polls provide the crucial information for decisions about how to spend money as the campaign progresses. If name recognition is not rising as fast as it should, then more money has to be spent on radio and television ads or direct mail that presents the candidate. This means raising more money or spending it faster than desired, which means holding more fund-raisers. If attacks by the opponent are working, it is crucial to spend money on ads that counter the arguments being made. If the opponent's name recognition is rising and her negatives (unfavorable ratings) are not rising, it may be necessary to spend money defining her and attacking her. If the candidate's own party is not strongly supporting her, it is necessary to spend money on direct mail to those in her party to get a very specific message to them. If the candidate is male, and he is not doing well among women, it will help to send letters from prominent women supporters to just women. All this takes money, and there is no reason to conduct the polls unless the campaign is prepared to respond by raising money and spending it.

Every campaign faces the issue of how often to poll. Ideally a campaign will poll every two to three weeks in September and October, so it can track the success of the campaign plan. If polling is done regularly, it is possible to have a greater sense of the impact of critical ads or statements by the opponent, and of newspaper stories. Without regular polling, estimating these effects is more difficult, since it is not possible to be certain about what might be the source of change from a month ago. Without that information, it is more difficult to know what to respond to. Is a candidate sliding because of his general persona and presentation or because of the opponent's ads of two weeks ago? The other difficulty with the timing of polling is that campaigns often wish to hold off on polling until they have run their own ads or until the opponent has run his ads. The goal is to know the precise effect of both kinds of ads. Very often it is not possible to know when ads will be run. This often makes it difficult to know when to poll.

Coping with the Unexpected

Most campaigns experience unexpected events. Candidates make misstatements and lose their temper, old voting records are published by the newspaper, and campaign funds are accepted from the "wrong" interest group. Campaigns often need to know the effect of these matters, so they can know whether to ignore it or respond. This can lead to very short tracking polls—name recognition, the matchup, and then questions such as "what do you remember hearing, seeing, or reading about the campaign in the last week," followed by "did that make you more or less positive toward _____?" These polls can be conducted a few days after the event, to give people time to find out about it and think about it, and then turned around overnight to let the campaign know if there is something they should do.

As with reports in general, reports about tracking polls should be organized to answer the questions the campaign manager has: what trends are occurring in name recognition and the matchup, how are issues playing a role, and what effect have events had.

The Undecided

Undecided voters are often crucial in a campaign, because how they break may decide a campaign. The difficult matter is to try to determine how they might vote. There are several ways to try to deal with them. The simplest way to deal with the undecided is to probe, after the first matchup question, for whether they lean to either candidate. Those who are left are either undecided or unwilling to tell the caller their choice. This may still leave a substantial percentage of likely voters who have not indicated how they will vote.

The next step is to try to predict the likely behavior of those left as undecided. First, these may be people who really are undecided, and many of them may not vote. One way to assess this possibility is to examine overall turnout in past elections and compare this percentage with the result of the decisions made in pulling a sample. If only 50 percent of registrants vote in similar elections, and the sampling process drew a sample from the 70 percent of all registrants most likely to vote, then it may be that the sampling is including some people with limited interest and they may not vote. If the undecided have a record of voting less and are Independents, it is possible that they will not vote. If so, the likely outcome should be calculated among only those with a choice.

The other alternative is to examine who the undecided are. If most of them have the same party registration and political views as the candidate, it might be presumed that they will vote for the candidate. Sometimes campaigns faced with a close election include questions about reactions to the parties and the personal image of candidates to see if those undecided are favorable to the candidate or his party on several traits, suggesting that they might lean to the party candidate. The danger with this approach is that it can be dangerous to the survival of incumbents. Some argue that those without an opinion are more likely to be less informed, more alienated, and less sympathetic to incumbents. For these reasons, many campaigns proceed on the presumption that the undecided will support the challenger. This is a more cautious assumption and puts the focus of the campaign on making sure that the incumbent is the choice of at least 51 percent of the sample. If the party registration and views of the undecided are more favorable to the opponent, it is best to assume they will vote for the opponent unless some steps are made to try to affect that outcome. If most are Republican, and the candidate is a Democrat, it is prudent to assume that the undecided are likely to vote Republican.

The most ambiguous situation is one in which the undecided look just like the pool of all voters: the percentages that are Republican and Democratic are just like the entire sample, and their views do not differ much. It is very difficult to know how the undecided will vote in such a situation. Pollsters and campaigns spend a great deal of time analyzing and discussing the undecided. In these situations the conversations are generally unsatisfactory, with the campaign manager asking that the pollster let him know if he can find any pattern to predict how they will vote. Very often there is nothing to tell the campaign other than that they look like the overall sample. The undecided often remain an unknown that forces the campaign to keep running television and radio ads and sending direct mail in the hope that the undecided will not break against the candidate.

A Final Note on Polling and Democracy   10

W E HAVE HIGH EXPECTATIONS about how campaigns contribute to democracy. During the course of campaigns, we
hope that:

- Candidates are forced to present themselves so the electorate has
  some idea of what they are like.
- Candidates present their positions on public policies that the
  electorate cares about.
- Incumbents have their record scrutinized by challengers so there
  is a review of their record.
- There is some debate of issues and alternatives so the electorate
  has some choice.

Polling contributes to this process in numerous ways. It contributes to campaigns with a focus on public concerns. Polling provides
information to candidates about the views of the electorate and what
issues are most important to them. When polling is used, candidates
do not conduct campaigns unaware of what concerns are most important to voters. Candidates are then likely to have greater sensitivity to
the concerns of voters, and they are likely to focus on the issues of
greatest concern to voters.

What do they do with this greater knowledge? Do they pander to
the public or do they try to manipulate the public? In reality their
responses are much more diverse than this. Sometimes they respond
to the public (pander). Sometimes they try to shape the way the
debate is seen (manipulate). Sometimes they realize the electorate
does not recognize a problem and they must take time to build support for a decision. Sometimes they realize that the electorate does not
like a solution, and they must either explain it or hope that before the
next election events develop in a way that indicates their decision is

working out well. Polling information allows them to decide how to handle each situation.

The national parties each provide an example of responding (called pandering by some). In 1996 the Republicans had won control of Congress and wanted to change the rules regarding welfare. Up to that point welfare recipients could stay on the rolls as long as they wished. The Republicans wanted a limit of two years at any time and a total of five years over a lifetime. Many Democrats did not want to vote for this, but public opinion polls indicated clear support for these kinds of limits. Some Democrats indicated that they thought that imposing these limits would eliminate this as an issue for awhile, and they voted for the changes. Given that a majority of Americans wanted these limits, and that the party sensed that they were in a precarious situation following the Republican takeover of Congress after the 1994 elections, the party responded. Their core constituency did not like the changes, but the majority of voters did.

The Republicans faced a situation equally difficult to resist in 2002. As discussed earlier, with corporate scandals dominating the news, the economy not growing, and the stock market falling, Republicans found it very difficult to vote against tougher penalties for corporate officials engaging in illegal financial activities, so they voted for them. Their core constituency did not like the changes, but the majority of voters did.

Other times the response of politicians is to try to shape the debate by articulating the debate in language they see as most appropriate. This is defined as manipulating by some. If crime is a serious concern, a conservative is likely to see the situation as an opportunity to present his conservative vision of what should be done about the problem. A liberal may be inclined to see this as an opportunity to make the case for the cumulative effects of poverty, dilapidated housing, and bad schools. When health care became an important issue at the beginning of the Clinton presidency, the rising prominence of this issue did not lead conservatives to agree with Clinton. Rather, it lead them to try to figure out, using polling, how to present their case about health care to the voters. The result is that candidates are aware of public concerns and focus on how to present their notion of how to address a problem.

Other times polling indicates that the public has little sense of a problem that is developing. A government may face a fiscal problem and need to cut programs or raise taxes. The poll information is crucial to let the officials be aware of the situation they face. They either need to wait longer and allow more stories about the seriousness of the problem to emerge before they act, or they need to establish a plan for going to numerous public meetings to explain their actions. Polling then lets them know how opinion is evolving.

All these uses of polling occur, and their usage varies over time. To present polling as contributing to pandering (responding) or manipulating (shaping an argument) is just too simple and distant from the day-to-day realities that officials face.

Polling also contributes to the accountability of incumbents towards their constituents. Incumbents have a means of obtaining feedback on what they do and how they are seen. They can ask whether the public also supports positions they support. Polling tells them whether positions they are adopting are different from the majority of their constituents. If an incumbent feels that she must do something that is unpopular—veto or cut a popular program, raise taxes, oppose a nomination—the polling will tell her how serious the public opposition is and how the public sees the issue. They are unlikely to change their views, but the polling provides them information about the need to explain their views to gain some acceptance of them.

Polling also provides a means for challengers to hold incumbents accountable. They can select specific policy positions of the incumbent that they think are divergent from the views of the district, test for voter acceptance, and make an issue of that position during a campaign. Incumbents know that, and it makes them very aware of how much they need to prepare the public for decisions they make and about the need to explain why they have made specific decisions. They have to respect the public, acknowledge how little the public may follow issues, and have a plan to communicate to the public. If they do not do that, they will lose support and votes. Polling provides them with a means to sense how the public sees them, their policies, and the political debates. That interaction cannot help but enhance democracy.

APPENDIX: A SAMPLE REPORT

THE FOLLOWING IS A REPORT presented to a candidate for district attorney. Some background is important for understanding the report. Sam Jackson had held the position of district attorney for a long time. Rumors had circulated for a while that he might resign, but no one had any definite information. Several prominent local attorneys had positioned themselves for a run if Jackson resigned. Jackson then resigned abruptly, and a very quick meeting of Democratic Party officials was held to choose a candidate for the November elections. The party chose between Jack Murphy and Mike Smith and selected Murphy. There were numerous rumors that Jackson had resigned and negotiated a deal that Murphy would get the nomination.

Smith was then approached by the Republicans about running on their line. He agreed, and then a poll was done to assess public perceptions of the entire process and Smith's prospects of beating Murphy in the November election.

Summary and Recommendations

About 50 percent of registrants have followed the resignation of Jackson and the selection of a candidate for November, and 50 percent of the registrants believe there was a deal. There is clearly a basis for emphasizing that something inappropriate has occurred with this process.

On the other hand, 50 percent do not think there was a deal. Murphy has emerged from this process without high negatives. It is necessary for the Republican campaign to connect Murphy to this whole process in a negative way. His favorable–unfavorable ratio is higher among those who followed the situation. He wins the matchup among those who have followed it. Further, only 12 percent believe there was a deal to go easy in prosecuting politicians.

It will not be possible to win this election by just stressing that something wrong has happened and stressing credentials. The campaign must remind voters of the process that resulted and make it clear that Murphy has to be a party to that process and any deal that was made.

Further, it is crucial to present the deal as a compromise of the fairness of the office (who is and who is not prosecuted) and not just as a deal among ambitious politicians to control who is next. I doubt that such a theme will grab the attention of voters and make enough Democrats abandon their own party. This theme is particularly important because about 30 percent of voters find Mike's acceptance of the Republican line opportunistic. This can be responded to by stressing that the deal will compromise the integrity of the office, and it is only to preserve integrity that Mike was willing to abandon his party.

It is very possible to win this race, despite the heavy Democratic enrollment. Most people have not followed this process closely. But there is plenty of media material to feed voters to define what happened. Most voters do not know the candidates, so there is an excellent opportunity to tell them who Jack Murphy is.

The themes I would stress, then, are:

- The process of resignation and selection of a Democratic candidate suggests that something corrupt is occurring.
- The result is likely to be corruption of the fairness of prosecutions in the DA's office. Not only have the people been cheated, but the deal that accompanied that will have real consequences for how much we can trust the DA.
- Mike is willing to run to preserve the integrity of the DA office. He promises fair treatment for all and independence from political bosses. Do you want someone who owes party bosses, or someone independent?

Following the Issue and Perceptions of a Deal

Jackson's resignation and the process of selecting Murphy and Smith were followed by 57 percent of all registrants (table A.1). Of those registrants, 19 percent said they followed it a lot, while 39 percent said they followed it somewhat; 52 percent of all registrants think there was some sort of deal among politicians. Perception of the existence of a deal is heavily associated with how much voters followed the issue. Of those who followed it a lot, 77 percent think there was a deal. Of those following it somewhat, 59 percent think there was a deal. Of those who did not follow it, 33 percent think there was a deal. As awareness declines, the percentage choosing no deal stays at around 20 and the percentage with no opinion increases.

There are two crucial matters here. Those who followed it think there was a deal. But a large segment did not follow it much. The first group reports they vote regularly, so it is only necessary to reinforce their views. The latter group does not report that they vote as frequently. They are probably less attentive to politics, and the campaign must present them with an interpretation of what happened, which may persuade them that something inappropriate took place.

Table A.1   Following the Issue

Q 6. How much have you followed the stories about the district attorney situation—Jackson's resignation, and the subsequent process of selecting party candidates for a November election—a lot, only somewhat, or not much at all.

A lot	18.7
Only somewhat	38.5
Not much	39.5
No response	3.3

Q 11. Critics charge that the timing of Jackson's resignation and Murphy's nomination by the Democrats was the result of a deal among politicians. Murphy's supporters dispute the existence of any deal and say the normal process of nomination for when a DA resigns abruptly played out. Do you think there was some deal or a normal process?

A deal	52.1
Normal process	17.1
No opinion	30.8

We also asked an open-ended question: "When you think of how this has developed, what comes to mind?" The responses (table A.2) also indicate the split in reactions between those who think it was a

deal and those who don't know much about it. The responses broke
down as follows.

Table A.2   Open-Ended Responses

Voter Expressions	Number
"a deal / backroom politics / a plot / something sneaky / violation of process"	105
"don't know enough / not sure what happened"	87
"time for Jackson to go / did a good job"	19
no comment offered at all	90

About one-third of the respondents (105 out of 301) mentioned
that something shady had occurred, while 87 said they did not know
enough and another 90 made no comment at all. Almost 60 percent
explicitly indicated that either they did not know enough about the
situation or they had nothing to offer. Again, there is a substantial proportion of voters who must be provided with an interpretation of what
happened.

While there is a substantial proportion who thinks there was a deal,
it will be necessary to create a sense of what that deal might involve.
When voters were asked if they think a deal might have been cut to go
easy on prosecuting politicians (table A.3), only 12 percent believe
that such an agreement was reached. Among those who followed the
situation a lot, this percentage is only 11. Among those who think
there was a deal, only 18 percent think that an agreement about
leniency was reached. It will not be enough to just allude to a deal.
The nature of the deal and its implications for trust in the DA's fairness
must be made an explicit charge. It appears that most voters do not
think some deal was made that would compromise the fairness of the
DA's office. They may think a deal involved just serving the ambitions
of politicians and not some more fundamental issue. The existence of
a deal, the terms of such a deal, and the implications for fairness have
to be made an issue. As of now, 46 percent have no opinion about
whether such a deal may have been arranged. It is necessary to convince them that something happened.

There is clearly support for making an issue of prosecuting white-
collar crime and politicians. A large majority (69 percent) think that
white-collar crimes and politicians should be prosecuted more. This
opinion is widely shared among all groups, with Independents particularly high on this (80 percent). If enough voters can be convinced that

there was a deal involving prosecution priorities, it could move many of them to not vote for Murphy and to vote for Mike.

Table A.3   Prosecution Issues

Q 12. Some have speculated that there is a deal that Murphy will go easy on prosecuting politicians. Do you believe that or not?

Believe	12.0
Don't believe	41.9
No opinion	46.0

Q 13. Sam Jackson often said that he didn't have the resources to prosecute white-collar crimes and political corruption and that other crimes were more pressing. Should these cases receive more attention or should they remain a secondary concern?

More attention	68.5
Secondary	17.0
No opinion	14.5

Name Recognition and Ratings

Murphy has somewhat of an edge in name recognition (table A.4). Just 43 percent have never heard of Murphy, while 58 percent have never heard of Mike. Despite that, Murphy does not have a significant advantage in ratings. His favorable–unfavorable rating is only somewhat more favorable than Mike's.

Awareness of the resignation and perceptions of the situation have only a limited impact on either Mike or Murphy. Among those following the issue a lot, Murphy's ratings are 43 to 13, while Mike's are 39 to 11. Among those who think there was a deal, Murphy is 19 to 6, while Mike is 22 to 5. Neither candidate has come out of this process with negative images among those who have followed the issue. Neither candidate has a negative image among those who think there was a deal. It is necessary to connect Murphy to the process to tell voters about his association. Otherwise, he will be able to run ads that simply present his credentials, and the Democratic Party enrollment advantage will provide a sufficient basis for him to win. It is also necessary to provide a reason why they should worry about his connection.

There is limited variation by party enrollment or sex in name recognition and ratings for either Murphy or Mike (table A.5). Both are

Table A.4 Candidate Name Recognition and Ratings

	Favorable	Unfavorable	No Opinion	Never Heard Of
Mike Smith	16.6	5.0	21.2	57.3
Jack Murphy	21.2	5.3	30.5	43.0
Al Gore	61.6	30.8	7.6	—
George W. Bush	42.4	48.3	8.9	0.3
Sam Jackson	52.6	24.5	17.2	5.6

better known among Democrats, and Murphy has a slight advantage among this group. But both candidates are largely unknown among the electorate and have considerable potential to fill out their image in the next month.

Table A.5 Name Recognition and Ratings by Groups

	Favorable	Unfavorable	No Opinion	Never Heard Of
Mike Smith				
Party				
Republicans	14.4	7.9	30.0	47.8
Independents (B)	12.1	6.9	31.0	50.0
Democrats	29.3	3.4	29.9	37.4
Sex				
Female	17.3	6.2	27.8	48.8
Male	25.2	3.1	35.9	35.9
Jack Murphy				
Party				
Republicans	13.3	1.1	24.4	61.1
Independents (B)	15.5	5.2	13.8	65.5
Democrats	18.4	6.8	23.1	51.7
Sex				
Female	18.5	4.9	19.1	57.4
Male	13.0	5.3	25.2	56.5

The open-ended comments on Murphy and Smith provide further evidence that neither Murphy nor Mike has a clear image (table A.6). Most indicated they don't know them. For Murphy, the most positive comments involved a recall of something he had done or his family. Mike received more comments involving his past prosecutions, but they are still a small percentage of the sample. Both are largely unknown.

Table A.6   Open-Ended Comments

Murphy		Smith	
Bad situation / process	12	Maverick / bad Democrat	4
Recognize him—Democrat / DA office	13	Positive—good guy / competency	49
Positive—good guy, good family / father	61	Brave to enter race	7
Don't know / nothing comes to mind	119	Don't know / nothing	166
No comment at all	97	No comment at all	70

The Matchup

Right now Murphy wins a matchup 34 to 27, with leaners added in (table A.7). Murphy wins Democrats 46 to 20, and Mike wins Independents 30 to 25 and Republicans 37 to 17. The problem is Democrats constitute 52 percent of the county, and the advantage Murphy has among them provides a margin. Given the enrollment advantage of a Democratic candidate, it is not enough to just rely on winning Republicans and Independents. It is crucial to try to bring down Murphy's proportion among Democrats, and that can only be done by criticizing him for a deal with Republicans and for protecting certain people.

Table A.7   Matchup

Q 3. This November there will be an election for Albany County district attorney. The choices are Jack Murphy, the Democratic Party candidate, and Mike Smith, the candidate of the Republican and Conservative Parties. Would you most likely vote for Murphy or Smith? (*If no choice*: "as of today would you lean to Murphy or Smith?")

Initial Responses		With Leaners Added	
Murphy	25.2	Murphy	33.5
Lean Murphy	8.3	Smith	26.6
Lean Smith	7.0	No Choice	39.9
Smith	19.6		
No choice	39.9		

More men indicate they have decided. They are 37 to 29 for Murphy, with 34 percent undecided. Women are 31 to 25, with 44 percent undecided. Getting a message to women that something corrupt has happened and appealing to concerns about fairness could produce a solid movement to Mike.

Those who followed the situation a lot are 43 percent Murphy to

34 percent Mike, while those following it only somewhat are 30 to 31. Those who have not paid much attention are 36 percent Murphy to 21 percent Mike. This last group is substantial (40 percent of registrants), and getting an interpretation of events to them is crucial.

The Crossing Party Lines Issue and Independence

If there is one issue that could harm Mike's image, it is the issue of crossing party lines to run (table A.8). We asked directly about that. About 30 percent find this questionable and opportunistic, while 50 percent do not regard it as an important matter. The greatest concern about this is among Democrats (38 percent questionable to 40 percent no opinion). The good news is that concern about this is lower among Independents (27 to 52) and Republicans (19 to 65), the two groups that Mike has to have to win.

Women (36 percent questionable to 41 percent not important) are more troubled about this than men (24 to 59). If women are to be won over, it is necessary to provide them with a compelling reason for why Mike is accepting the Republican line. This situation provides an opportunity to present an explanation of the deal, its consequences for fairness in the DA's office, and a compelling reason why Mike would

Table A.8   Crossing Party Lines and Independence

Q 10. Smith has been a life-long Democrat, but is running as the Republican candidate. Do you see his crossing party lines as questionable and opportunistic or not an important matter?

Questionable	29.8
Not important	49.7
No opinion	20.5

Q 15. Which of the candidates do you think will be most independent in making decisions about what crimes to prosecute, Murphy or Smith?

Murphy	11.8
Smith	21.5
No opinion	66.7

cross party lines. His candidacy is an act to try to preserve fairness in the prosecution of laws. It, again, provides an opportunity to criticize Murphy.

This issue has considerable impact in how people are voting at this stage. Those who find crossing party lines questionable are 49 percent Murphy to 14 percent Mike. Those who do not regard it as important are 28 percent Murphy to 37 percent Mike. It is important to solidify support among those not seeing this as important by providing an explanation. An explanation will also help persuade the 20 percent without an opinion that Mike has a reason for doing this, which will increase his general level of support.

At this point more people think Mike will have greater independence. This advantage, while important, is small, and it must be much greater by November 7. If Mike can tie together a theme of inside deals, corruption of the office with differential treatment, and his concern for the integrity of the office, he can increase the perception that he is independent. This will help a great deal. These opinions about independence have a powerful impact on vote choices. Those who see Murphy as most independent go for him 91 to 3, while those who see Mike as independent go for Mike 53 to 18. It is crucial, particularly for this office, to build an image of independence.

Qualifications

Given how little voters know about Murphy and Mike, it is not surprising that there are few who have an opinion as to who is most qualified and they think there is little difference between the two (table A.9). About 80 percent have no opinion, and among those with an opinion, there is little difference. It is important to stress credentials, so Murphy does not gain an advantage in this area, but this is unlikely to be central to this campaign. Further, given the limited time available, the way this situation has developed, and the limited funds likely to be available, the emphasis must be on the issues of process, deals, corruption, and independence. There is not enough time or money to spend a great deal of resources on establishing credentials. They must be there, but not as the central focus. If this is a contest waged on credentials, with two candidates both having roughly equal credentials, partisan voting will take over, and Murphy will win because there are more Democrats.

Table A.9 Qualifications

Q 14. Which of these candidates—Murphy and Smith—do you think is most qualified to be district attorney, or do you not know enough to judge that?

Murphy	10.4
Smith	8.7
Don't know enough	81.0

The Possible Role of Dissatisfactions

While the next month will likely focus on how this situation developed, there are also likely to be more general and traditional concerns about the past and future of the DA's office. There may be concerns about crime, about how the DA's office has performed, and about the relationship with the police. We asked about all those issues (table A.10). There does not appear to be much concern that crime is increasing, with only 20 percent indicating that they see crime increasing. There also does not appear to be any obvious dissatisfaction with the DA's office. Only 17 percent indicate they are dissatisfied, though a little over one-third indicate they don't know enough to judge the issue. It does not appear that there is enough concern about crime and how the DA's office has performed to use these as issues. Despite the limited dissatisfaction with the current situation, Mike does appear to benefit from whatever dissatisfaction does exist. Those who see an increase in crime are Murphy 30 percent to Mike 32 percent, while those who see no change are 35 to 27. The difference is small, but at least Mike begins with a slight advantage of being seen as a better alternative to those worried about crime. The same pattern exists regarding approval of the DA's office. Those who approve are 39 percent Murphy to 26 percent Mike, while those disapproving are 20 percent Murphy to 33 percent Mike. Again, Mike is seen as an alternative for those with dissatisfactions. While it is difficult to criticize an office where Mike has worked, he can express his concerns about making some changes.

Finally, there is the issue of the relationship with the police. This divides the public, but it does not play a role at this point in vote choices. Those who see a union endorsement as positive will vote for Murphy at the same rate as those who think it could be a sign of being too cozy with the police. This issue is unlikely to be of use in a short campaign.

Table A.10   Issue Questions

Q 16. In recent years, has crime in your neighborhood increased, decreased, or stayed about the same?

Increased	19.7
Same	70.9
Decreased	6.9
No opinion	2.4

Q 17. Do you generally approve or disapprove of the job the district attorney's office has done in recent years in prosecuting crime, or do you not know enough to judge that?

Approve	43.3
Disapprove	17.0
Don't know	37.0
No opinion	2.8

Q 18. Do you see an endorsement by a police union as a sign of the capability of a district attorney candidate, or a sign that the DA may be too cozy with the police and unwilling to prosecute police corruption?

Capability	29.1
Too cozy	31.8
No opinion	39.1

The Presidential and Senate Races

The presidential and Senate races may well play a role in affecting partisan voting (table A.11). Both Gore and Hillary Clinton are winning in the county. This could pull many voters to vote Democratic and help Murphy. While that is possible, there are several reasons why this may not be a problem. Support for Gore and Clinton are clearly not that strong, and they may not pull many voters. The crosstabs also indicate that those who are voting for Gore and Clinton are willing to split their ticket.

Calling and the Sample

Calling took place October 2–6. An initial list of names and telephone numbers was obtained from Survey Sampling, Inc. About 300 registrants were contacted. Since 2000 will be a presidential year in the election cycle, voter turnout could be high, so we did not use any

Table A.11   Presidential and Senate Races

Q 12. In the presidential election this November, will you most likely vote for George Bush, the Republican, or Al Gore, the Democrat?

Bush	31.6
Gore	48.8
Undecided	19.6

Q 13. In the New York Senate election in November, will you most likely vote for Rick Lazio, the Republican, or Hillary Clinton, the Democrat?

Clinton	47.3
Lazio	39.3
Undecided	13.3

screening. We did ask how frequently people vote, and results by differences by voting frequency are reported.

The table below (table A.12) presents the profile of the county, based on the SSI sample and those we contacted. The profiles represent percentages, and they sum down within each group. For example, within the county, of all registrants, 52 percent are Democrats, 20 percent are Independents, and 25 percent are Republicans. The percentages for party enrollment from the SSI sample are very similar to those available as of now for Warren County and can be found on the State Board of Elections web page.

The profile of those we contacted is shown in the second column. The crucial matter is whether the sample is representative of registered voters.

The script used for the poll follows.

Table A.12   Comparison of County Registrants and Sample Percent Distribution

	County	Those Contacted
Party		
Republicans	24.7	30.0
Independents	20.3	19.3
Democrats	51.6	49.0
Sex		
Female	53.0	54.5
Male	47.0	45.5

Survey Script

Hello, may I please speak with _____.

My name is _____. I'm calling from Opinion Research. We're not selling anything. We're conducting a survey in this area this evening, and I wonder if I might have a few minutes of your time?

1. Generally speaking, are things in the Albany area headed in the right direction, or in the wrong direction?

   1 ____ right direction   2 ____ wrong direction   3 ____ no opinion

2. I'd like to read you the names of some people in public life. For each name, could you please tell me whether your impressions of that person are favorable or unfavorable. If you have never heard of someone, or don't know enough to rate the person, just say so.

Table A.13   Impression of Public Figures

	Favorable	Unfavorable	No Opinion	Never Heard Of
Al Gore	1	2	3	4
George W. Bush	1	2	3	4
Jack Murphy	1	2	3	4
Mike Smith	1	2	3	4
Sam Jackson	1	2	3	4

3. This November there will be an election for Warren County district attorney. The choices are Jack Murphy, the Democratic Party candidate, and Mike Smith, the candidate of the Republican and Conservative Parties. Would you most likely vote for Murphy or Smith?

   (If no choice: "As of today would you lean to Murphy or Smith?")

   1 ____ Murphy   2 ____ lean Murphy   3 ____ lean Smith
   4 ____ Smith   5 ____ no choice

4. In the presidential election, will you most likely vote for George W. Bush, the Republican candidate, or Al Gore, the Democratic candidate?

   1 ____ Bush   2 ____ Gore   3 ____ no choice

5. In the election for U.S. Senator from New York, would you vote for Hillary Clinton, the Democratic and Working Families Party's candidate, or Rick Lazio, the Republican and Conservative Party's candidate?

   1 ____ Clinton   2 ____ Lazio   3 ____ no choice

6. How much have you followed the stories about the district attorney situation—Jackson's resignation, and the subsequent process of selecting party candidates for a November election—a lot, only somewhat, or not much at all?
1 ___ a lot   2 ___ only somewhat   3 ___ not much
4 ___ no response

7. When you think of how this has developed, what comes to mind?
_____

8. When you think of Jack Murphy, what comes to mind? _____

9. When you think of Mike Smith, what comes to mind? _____

10. Smith has been a life-long Democrat, but is running as the Republican candidate. Do you see his crossing party lines as questionable and opportunistic or not an important matter?
1 ___ questionable   2 ___ not important   3 ___ no opinion

11. Critics charge that the timing of Jackson's nomination and Murphy's nomination by the Democrats was the result of a deal among politicians. Murphy's supporters dispute the existence of any deal and say the normal process of nomination when a DA resigns abruptly played out. Do you think there was some deal or a normal process?
1 ___ deal   2 ___ normal   3 ___ no opinion

12. Some have speculated that there is a deal that Murphy will go easy on prosecuting politicians. Do you believe that or not?
1 ___ believe   2 ___ don't believe   3 ___ no opinion

13. Sam Jackson often said that he didn't have the resources to prosecute white-collar crimes and political corruption and that other crimes were more pressing. Should these cases receive more attention or should they remain a secondary concern?
1 ___ more attention   2 ___ secondary   3 ___ no opinion

14. Which of these candidates—Murphy and Smith—do you think is most qualified to be district attorney, or do you not know enough to judge that?
1 ___ Murphy   2 ___ Smith   3 ___ no opinion

15. Which of the candidates do you think will be most independent in making decisions about what crimes to prosecute, Murphy or Smith?
   1 ___ Murphy   2 ___ Smith   3 ___ no opinion

16. In recent years, has crime in your neighborhood increased, decreased, or stayed about the same?
   1 ___ increased   2 ___ same   3 ___ decreased
   4 ___ no opinion

17. Do you generally approve or disapprove of the job the district attorney's office has done in recent years in prosecuting crime, or do you not know enough to judge that?
   1 ___ approve   2 ___ disapprove   3 ___ don't know
   4 ___ no opinion

18. Do you see an endorsement by a police union as a sign of the capability of a district attorney candidate, or a sign that the DA may be too cozy with the police and unwilling to prosecute police corruption?
   1 ___ capability   2 ___ too cozy   3 ___ no opinion

19. Do you generally regard yourself as liberal, moderate, or conservative, or do none of those apply?
   1 ___ liberal   2 ___ moderate   3 ___ conservative   4 ___ none

20. Do you tend to vote always, most of the time, or just sometimes?
   1 ___ always   2 ___ most of the time   3 ___ just sometimes
   4 ___ no response

21. Do you tend to vote mostly for Democrats, mostly for Republicans, or do you split your vote?
   1 ___ Democrats   2 ___ Republicans   3 ___ Split
   4 ___ no response

22. Is your age 18–29, 30–44, 45–59, or 60 plus?
   1 ___ 18–29   2 ___ 30–44   3 ___ 45–59
   4 ___ 60 plus   5 ___ no answer

23. Into which of the following categories does your annual family income fall? *(Read categories.)*
    1 ___ Under $25,000
    2 ___ $ 25–49,000
    3 ___ $ 50–74,000
    4 ___ $ 75,000 or more
    5 ___ Don't know / refused

That completes the survey. Thanks for participating.

BIBLIOGRAPHY

General Bibliography

Abramowitz, Alan I. 1994. "Issue Evolution Reconsidered: Racial Attitudes and Partisanship in the U.S. Electorate." *American Journal of Political Science* 38, No. 1 (February): 1–24.

Abramowitz, Alan I. and Kyle L. Saunders. 1998. "Ideological Realignments in the U.S. Electorate." *Journal of Politics* 60, No. 3 (August): 634–52.

———. 2000. "Ideological Realignment and U.S. Congressional Elections." Paper presented at the Annual Meeting of the American Political Science Association, Washington, D.C., September.

Asher, Herbert. 1992. *Polling and the Public.* 2nd Edition. Washington, D.C.: C.Q. Press.

Bartells, Larry M. 2000. "Partisanship and Voting Behavior, 1952–1996." *American Journal of Political Science* 44, No. 1 (January): 35–49.

Benton, J. Edwin and John L. Daly. 1991. "A Question Order Effect in a Local Government Survey." *Public Opinion Quarterly.* Vol. 55: 640–42.

Berry, Frances S. and William D. Berry. 1990. "State Lottery Adoptions as Policy Innovations: An Event History Analysis." *American Political Science Review.* Vol. 84, No. 2 (June): 395–417.

Blais, Andre, Neil Nevitte, Elisabeth Gidengil, and Richard Nadeau. 2000. "Do People Have Feelings Toward Leaders About Whom They Say They Know Nothing?" *Public Opinion Quarterly.* Vol. 64: 452–63.

Bolstein, Richard. 1991. "Comparison of the Likelihood to Vote among Preelection Poll Respondents and Nonrespondents." *Public Opinion Quarterly.* Vol. 55: 648–50.

Breaux, David A. and Anthony Gierzynski. 1991. "'It's Money that Matters': Campaign Expenditures and State Legislative Primaries." *Legislative Studies Quarterly.* Vol. 16, No. 3 (August): 429–44.

Brewer, Mark D. 2003. *Relevant No More? The Catholic/Protestant Divide in American Electoral Politics.* Lexington, Mass: Lexington Books.

Brewer, Mark D. and Jeffrey M. Stonecash. 2001. "Class, Race Issues, Declining White Support for the Democratic Party in the South." *Political Behavior.* Vol. 23, No. 2 (June): 131–55.

Brick, J. Michael, Joseph Waksberg, Dale Kulp, and Amy Starer. 1995. "Bias in

List-Assisted Telephone Samples." *Public Opinion Quarterly*. Vol. 59: 218–35.

Bumiller, Elisabeth. 2002. "Looking to Elections, Bush Plays Up Domestic Issues." *The New York Times*. May 10. A1.

Carmines, Edward G. and James A. Stimson. 1989. *Issue Evolution: Race and the Transformation of American Politics*. Princeton, N.J.: Princeton University Press.

Converse, Philip. 1964. "The Nature of Belief Systems in Mass Publics." In *Ideology and Discontent*, edited by David Apter. New York: Free Press: 206–61.

———. 1970. "Attitudes and Non-Attitudes: Continuation of a Dialogue." In *The Quantitative Analysis of Social Problems*, edited by Edward Tufte, 168–89. Reading, Mass.: Addison-Wesley.

Couper, Mick P. 1997. "Survey Introductions and Data Quality." *Public Opinion Quarterly*. Vol. 61: 317–38.

Crespi, Irving. 1988. *Pre-election Polling: Sources of Accuracy and Error*. New York: Russell Sage Foundation.

Day, Jennifer C. and Avalaura L. Gaither. 2000. "Voting and Registration in the Election of November 1998." Washington, D.C: U.S. Department of Commerce, U.S. Census Bureau, Economics and Statistics Administration. August.

Drew, Elizabeth. 1999. "The Presidency," excerpted from the book, *The Corruption of American Politics*." www.thirdworld*traveler/Political_Corruption/ Presidency_CAP.html*

Dunlap, Riley E. 2002. "An Enduring Concern." *Public Perspective*. September/October: 10–14.

Dwyre, Diana and Jeffrey M. Stonecash. 1992. "Where's the Party: Changing State Party Organizations." *American Politics Quarterly*. Vol. 20, No. 4. (July): 326–44.

Erikson, Robert. 1993. "Counting Likely Voters in Gallup's Tracking Poll." *Public Perspective*. March/April: 22–23.

Finkel, Steven E., Thomas M. Guterbock, and Marian J. Borg. 1991. "Race-of-Interviewer Effects in a Preelection Poll: Virginia 1989." *Public Opinion Quarterly*. Vol. 55: 313–30.

Fishkin, James S. 1996. *The Voice of the People*. New Haven: Yale University Press.

Flanigan, William H. and Nancy H. Zingale. 2002. *Political Behavior of the American Electorate*. 10th Edition. Washington, D.C.: C.Q. Press.

Fowler, Floyd, Jr. 1992. "How Unclear Terms Affect Survey Data." *Public Opinion Quarterly*. Vol. 56: 218–31.

Freedman, Paul and Ken Goldstein. 1996. "Building a Probable Electorate from Preelection Polls: A Two-Stage Approach." *Public Opinion Quarterly*. Vol. 60: 547–87.

Geer, John G. 1991. "Do Open-Ended Questions Measure 'Salient' Issues?" *Public Opinion Quarterly*. Vol. 55: 360–70.

Giles, Michael W. and Anita Pritchard. 1985. "Campaign Expenditures and Legislative Elections in Florida," *Legislative Studies Quarterly*. Vol. 10, No. 1 (February): 71–88.

Gierzynski, Anthony. 1992. *Legislative Party Campaign Committees in the States*. Lexington: University of Kentucky Press.

Gierzynski, Anthony and David Breaux. 1991. "Money and Votes in State Legislative Elections." *Legislative Studies Quarterly*. Vol. 16, No. 3 (May): 203–18.

Gilljam, Mikael and Donald Granberg. "Should We Take Don't Know for an Answer?" *Public Opinion Quarterly*. Vol. 57: 348–57.

Granberg, Donald. 1985. "An Anomaly in Political Perception." *Public Opinion Quarterly*. Vol. 49: 504–16.

Groseclose, Tim, Steven D. Levitt, and James M. Snyder, Jr. 1999. "Comparing Interest Group Scores across Time and Chambers: Adjusted ADA Scores for the U.S. Congress." *American Political Science Review*. Vol. 93, No. 1 (March): 33–50.

Groves, Robert M., et al. 1988. *Telephone Survey Methodology*. New York: John Wiley.

Hallow, Ralph Z. 2002. "As Polling Goes, Bush Is No Clinton." *The Washington Times*. April 10. Taken from www.washtimes.com/national/20020410–31160712.htm

Horovitz, Bruce. 2002. "Trust." *USA Today*. July 16. 1–2.

Jacobs, Lawrence R. and Robert Y. Shapiro. 2000. *Politicians Don't Pander: Political Manipulation and the Loss of Democratic Responsiveness*. Chicago: University of Chicago Press.

Jacobson, Gary C. and Samuel Kernell. 1983. *Strategy and Choice in Congressional Elections*. 2nd Edition. New Haven: Yale University Press.

Jamieson, Amie, Hyon R. Shin, and Jennifer Day. 2002. "Voting and Registration in the Election of November 2000." Washington, D.C: U.S. Department of Commerce, U.S. Census Bureau, Economics and Statistics Administration. February.

Jones, Ruth S. and Thomas J. Borris. 1985. "Strategic Contributing in Legislative Campaigns: The Case of Minnesota," *Legislative Studies Quarterly*. Vol. 10, No. 1 (February): 89–105.

Kane, Emily W. and Laura J. Macaulay. 1993. "Interviewer Gender and Gender Attitudes." *Public Opinion Quarterly*. Vol. 57: 1–28.

Keeter, Scott, Carolyn Miller, Andrew Kohut, Robert Groves, and Stanley Presser. 2000. "Consequences of Reducing Nonresponse in a National Telephone Survey." *Public Opinion Quarterly*. Vol. 64: 125–48.

King, Anthony. 1997. "Running Scared." *The Atlantic Monthly*. (January): 41–61.

Layman, Geoffrey. 2001. *The Great Divide*. New York: Columbia University Press.

Link, Michael W. and Robert W. Oldendick. 1999. "Call Screening: Is It Really a Problem for Survey Research?" *Public Opinion Quarterly*. Vol. 63: 577–89.

Martin, Elizabeth and Anne E. Polivka. 1995. "Diagnostics for Redesigning Survey Questionnaires: Measuring Work in the Current Population Survey." *Public Opinion Quarterly*. Vol. 59: 547–67.

Patterson, Thomas E. 1994. *Out of Order*. New York: Vintage.

———. 2002. *The Vanishing Voter: Public Involvement in an Age of Uncertainty*. New York: Alfred E. Knopf.

Ross, Steven S. 2000. "Reporting the Horse Race: To Poll or Not to Poll?" taken from www.fathom.com/story/story_printable.jhtml?storyID = 35307

Saad, Lydia. 2002. "Much More Than Fighting Terrorism on Americans' Agenda for Congress: Social and Economic Concerns Rank Nearly as High." www.gallup.com/poll/releases/pr020502.asp?Version = p

Sanchez, Maria Elena and Giovanna Morchio. 1992. "Probing 'Don't Know' Answers: Effects on Survey Estimates and Variable Relationships." *Public Opinion Quarterly*. Vol. 56: 454–74.

Schuman, Howard and Stanley Presser. 1981. *Questions and Answers in Attitude Surveys: Experiments on Question Form*. New York: Academic Press.

Shaiko, Ronald H., Jeffrey M. Stonecash, Diana Dwyre, Mark O'Gorman, and James Vike. 1991. "Pre-Election Political Polling and the Non-Response Bias Issue." *International Journal of Public Opinion Research*. Vol. 3, No. 1 (March): 86–99.

Stonecash, Jeffrey M. 1988. "Working at the Margins: Campaign Finance and Party Strategy in New York Assembly Elections." *Legislative Studies Quarterly*. Vol. 13, No. 4 (November): 477–93.

———. 1994. "Chickens and Eggs, Money and Votes. What's the Question and Does It Matter?" Paper prepared for the Conference on Campaign Finance sponsored by the Committee for the Study of the American Electorate, Washington, D.C. July 29–30.

———. 2000. *Class and Party in American Politics*. Boulder, Colo.: Westview Press.

———. 2003. *The Emergence of State Government: Parties and New Jersey Politics, 1950–2000*. Cranbury, N.J.: Fairleigh-Dickinson University Press.

Stonecash, Jeffrey M. and Diana Dwyre. 1992. "Where's the Party: Changing State Party Organizations." *American Politics Quarterly*. Vol. 20, No. 3 (July): 326–44.

Stonecash, Jeffrey M. and Chao-Chi Shan. 1994. "Legislative Resources and Electoral Margins: The New York State Senate, 1950–1990." *Legislative Studies Quarterly*. Vol. 19, No. 1 (February): 79–93.

Stonecash, Jeffrey M. and Sara E. Keith. 1996. "Maintaining a Political Party: Providing and Withdrawing Party Campaign Funds." *Party Politics* 2, No. 2 (July): 313–28.

Stonecash, Jeffrey M. and Nicole Lindstrom. 1999. "Emerging Party Cleavages in the U.S. House of Representatives. *American Politics Quarterly*. Vol. 27, No. 1 (January): 58–88.

Stonecash, Jeffrey M., Mark D. Brewer, Mary P. McGuire, R. Eric Petersen, and

Lori Beth Way. 2000. "Class and Party: Secular Realignment and the Survival of Democrats outside the South." *Political Research Quarterly.* Vol. 43, No. 4 (December): 731–52.

Stonecash, Jeffrey M. and Mack D. Mariani. 2000. "Republican Gains in the House in the 1994 Elections: Class Polarization in American Politics." *Political Science Quarterly.* Vol. 115, No. 1 (Spring): 93–113.

Stonecash, Jeffrey M. and Andrew Milstein. 2001. "Parties and Taxes: The Emergence of Distributive Issues, 1950–2000." Presented at the 2001 Midwest Political Science Association Meetings, Chicago, Ill. April.

Stonecash, Jeffrey M., Mark D. Brewer, and Mack D. Mariani. 2002. *Diverging Parties: Social Change, Realignment, and Party Polarization.* Boulder, Colo.: Westview Press.

Voss, D. Stephen, Andrew Gelman, and Gary King. 1995. "Review: Preelection Survey Methodology." *Public Opinion Quarterly.* Vol. 59, No. 98–132.

Witt, Evans. 2002. "Necessary Embrace: The Public and the News Media." *Public Perspective.* July/August: 27–30.

Polling Books

Asher, Herbert. 2001. *Polling and the Public: What Every Citizen Should Know.* 5th Edition. Washington, D.C.: Congressional Quarterly Inc.

Crespi, Irving. 1989. *Public Opinion, Polls, and Democracy.* Boulder, Colo.: Westview Press.

Fink, Arlene. 1995. *How to Analyze Survey Data.* Beverly Hills, Calif.: Sage Publications.

———. 1995. *The Survey Kit.* Beverly Hills, Calif.: Sage Publications.

Fink, Arlene and Jacqueline Kosecoff. 1998. *How to Conduct Surveys: A Step-by-Step Guide.* 2nd Edition. Beverly Hills, Calif.: Sage Publications.

Fowler, Floyd J., Jr. 2002. *Survey Research Methods.* 3rd Edition. Beverly Hills, Calif.: Sage Publications.

Fowler, Floyd J., Jr. and Thomas W. Mangione. 1990. *Standardized Survey Interviewing: Minimizing Interviewer-Related Error.* Newbury Park, Calif.: Sage Publications.

Fowler, Floyd J., Jr. and Floyd Fowler. 1995. *Improving Survey Questions: Design and Evaluation.* Newbury Park, Calif.: Sage Publications.

Frey, James H. 1983. *Survey Research by Telephone.* Beverly Hills, Calif.: Sage Publications.

Lavrakas, Paul J. 1987. *Telephone Survey Methods: Sampling, Selection, and Supervision.* Newbury Park, Calif.: Sage Publications.

Moore, David W. 1995. *The Superpollsters: How They Measure and Manipulate Public Opinion in America.* 2nd Edition. New York: Four Walls Eight Windows Press.

Patten, Mildred L. 2001 *Questionnaire Research: A Practical Guide.* Los Angeles: Pyrczak Publishing.

Traugott, Michael W. and Paul J. Lavrakas. 2000. *The Voter's Guide to Election Polls.* 2nd Edition. New York: Chatham House Publishers.

Web Sources

Hamilton, William R. 1995. "Political Polling: From the Beginning to the Center of American Election Campaigns." *Campaigns and Elections American Style.* Boulder, Colo.: Westview Press. www.hbstaff.com/political.htm. This paper provides an overview. It is written by a principal in the polling firm Hamilton, Beattie, and Staff. They offer a number of interesting articles on polling at: www.hbstaff.com/library.htm

Push Polling in General and in the 2000 Presidential Election

General

For a general listing of articles on push polling, see www.wlu.ca/lispop/rres/push.htm. This website presents articles by newsprint journalists about specific cases of push polling, articles in magazines such as *Campaigns and Elections* and *Public Opinion*, and books about polling. It also lists other websites that address the issue of push polling.

The 2000 Presidential Election

ABC News. "McCain Accuses Bush of Unfair Tactics." abcnews.go.com/sections/politics/DailyNews/SC_000210.html

Bennett, James. February 22, 2000. "The 2000 Campaign: The Battleground; Evangelist Goes on the Attack to Help Bush." *The New York Times.* Final, Section A, 1.

Christian Science Monitor. "In-Your-Ear Politics." www.csmonitor.com/durable/2000/02/16/p.10s2.htm

CNN. February 10, 2000. "'Push Polling' Takes Center Stage in Bush-McCain South Carolina Fight; Dems Campaign in California." www.cnn.com/2000/ALLPOLITICS/ stories/02/10/campaign warp/

Corera, Gordon. February 18, 2000. "The Gloves Come Off." news.bbc.co.uk/hi/english/in_depth/Americas/2000/us_elections/election_ . . . / 647644.st

Cyberalert. February 11, 2000. "'Nastier' & 'Uglier' Thanks to Bush Push Polling; McCain 'Not a Hypocrite.'" www.mediaresearch.org/cyberalerts/2000/cyb20000211.asp

Greenberger, Scott S. and Ken Harman. February 12, 2000. "McCain Pulls Negative Ads; Bush Declines to Follow Suit." www.coxnews.com/2000/news/cox/021200_push.html

INDEX

abortion as issue, 36, 37, 97–100, 106
academic polling, 55
age as demographic, 60, 113
analysis of results: and crosstabs, 80–82, 110, 136; and frequencies, 79–80; and marginals, 81, 82, 102, 133

benchmarks and campaign plans, 22, 23
benchmark poll, 12, 22, 23, 79
budget, 6, 8, 11–15, 35, 43, 95, 101
Bush, George W., 1, 43, 114, 115

callers: and training, 73; and volunteers, 76
challengers, 11, 12, 21, 85, 87
class division, 48
Clinton, Bill, 1, 2, 5
Clinton, Hillary, 88
conservatives, 120
corporate scandals, 96, 115
credentials, 93, 94

D'Amato, Al, 87, 88
defining opponents, 129–31
democracy:
    role of polling, 141, 143
Democrats, 48, 54, 69, 70, 80–82, 84, 87, 89, 90, 92, 93, 97, 104, 105, 107–16
demographics, 48–50; bias, 73; reelection, 24, 33, 52, 87

dirty tactics, 42

economic development, 99
electorate, 61, 95, 121, 129, 141

focus groups, 4

health care and health insurance, 5, 8, 36

incumbents, 11, 12, 21, 31, 33, 85, 90, 121, 128, 136, 138, 141, 143
Independents, 70, 90, 105, 113, 122–23
information:
    and political ads, 6, 8, 9, 12–14, 24, 103, 120, 127–32, 134, 136–37, 139; and role in campaign, 8, 9, 10
informed ballot, 52–54
intensity of opinions, 33–34
issues: and connection to other issues, 100–103; and moving voters, 93–100; and specific district situations, 103–15

liberals, 120, 124

matchups, 21, 22, 30–33, 88, 89, 112, 117–21, 137
McCall, Carl, 13
minorities, 109
mobilization of voters, 103, 114

name recognition, 29, 30, 83–85, 87, 93, 117–19, 127–31, 136–37; and assessing role in matchup, 91–93; and candidates, 82–88; and incumbents, 85–88
no opinion issue, 32–33

off-year election, 61

pandering to electorate, 141–43
party organizations, 14
political behavior, 2
pollster, 27, 28, 34, 55, 66, 138–39; and ethics, ix–x
polling and democracy, 1–8. *See also* democracy
presidential election, 29, 60, 62, 63
primary emphasis, 16, 17
public utilities, 122–25
pull voters, 109, 110
push polling, 41

questions, polling: and alternatives presented to respondents, 38, 39; closed-ended, 50, 51; language, 34, 35, 42; open-ended, 50, 51, 121

recall, 132–33
registration, 62–64, 67, 69, 75, 81, 105
religion, 48
reports: contents, 117; examples, 118–26, 145–55

Republicans, 48, 49, 69, 70, 74, 80–82, 84–93, 97, 104, 105, 107–16
respondents, 76
Ronald Reagan, 2

sample, 59, 65–68, 77, 139; and representativeness, 68; and selecting, 65–68; and under campaigning, 65–68
schools, 38, 39, 40, 41, 54, 101, 102, 121–22
Schumer, Chuck, 87, 88
script for poll, 31, 55, 79, 112, 114; process of writing, 27–29
sequence of questions, 29–32
secondary emphasis, 17
Social Security, 36, 37
strengths and weaknesses, 46, 47
summary reports, 15–17, 21, 22, 24

taxes, 3, 4, 38, 101, 104, 105, 122, 124–26, 134–36
timing of polls, 12–15
tracking poll, 24, 25, 127–31, 136–37; and effects of ads and literature, 131–33; and matchup, 133–37
traits, 44, 45
turnout, 59
2000 Presidential Election, 43

undecided, 137–39

women, 106

ABOUT THE AUTHOR

Jeffrey M. Stonecash is professor and chair of political science at the Maxwell School, Syracuse University. His research focuses on political parties, their electoral bases, and their roles in shaping public policy debates. He has published in journals such as *American Political Science Review*, *American Politics Quarterly*, *Legislative Studies Quarterly*, *Political Behavior*, and *Political Research Quarterly*. He is the editor of *Governing New York State*, 4th edition, published in 2001. His most recent books are *Class and Party in American Politics* (2000), *Diverging Parties* (2002), and *The Emergence of State Government* (2003). He conducts polls and consults for political candidates, and has been professor-in-residence in the New York State Assembly Intern Program since 1984.